Introduction to
JAFFNA COOKERY

by

Sathanithi Somasekaram

© Sathanithi Somasekaram 1995

All rights reserved. No part of this book may be stored or reproduced in any form by any means without the prior permission of the publisher and the copyright holder.

Computer typesetting by Mr. S. Jeganmohan

ISBN: 955 - 9276 - 01 - 8

Published and Distributed by:

Arjuna Consulting Company Ltd.,
60, School Avenue, Station Road,
Dehiwala, Sri Lanka.
Tel/Fax: 738803
E-mail: arjunaco@slt.lk

Printed by Guneratne Offset Ltd,
235/10, Avissawella Road,
Orugodawatta,
Sri Lanka.

INTRODUCTION

Jaffna meals are known for their variety and distinct taste. However, the preparation of even the ordinary dishes such as thosai, kool and Pt.Pedro vadai remain something of a mystery to peopl from other communities. It is to remove this mystery and make it possible for any interested person to prepare a typical Jaffna meal that this book has been written. Perhaps it will also help people who have gone abroad and lost touch with traditional Jaffna cookery. The recipes are set out in simple, easy to follow point form.

The meals can be made hot and spicy or very mild, to suit individual tastes. The secret to a good curry is the curry powder. Guidelines are given to alter the strength as desired. Where special ingredients such as palmyra yam flour are included in a recipe, e.g. kool, and it is not available with your grocer, try the Katpaham outlets of the Palmyra Development Board.

This book is divided into fourteen sections, with an alphabetical index of all the recipes. Conversion tables for weights and measures, explanations for cooking terms, substitutes for some ingredients and Sinhala and Tamil equivalents are given immediately after the index. Suggested accompaniments for these meals are also given. Recipes for cakes and puddings have been included to make the book a more complete guide to cooking.

I wish to express my gratitude to my son-in-law S. Jeganmohan who took great pains in typesetting the book, B. Jeyanath, who drew the cover, Guneratne Offset Ltd who have undertaken the printing - and my husband T. Somasekaram who encouraged me to put my experience of 30 years in book form.

Mrs. Sathanithi Somasekaram

CONTENTS

Index	v
Conversion Tables	ix
Cooking Terms	x
Substitutes	xi
Equivalent Terms in Sinhala & Tamil	xii
Photographs	Between pp xii & 1
Breakfast	1
Suggested Accompaniments	14
Soups	15
Rice Recipes	21
Flour	29
Curry Powders	32
Curries	37
Sea Foods	39
Egg and Meat	53
Vegetables	65
Sambals, Pachchadis and Chutneys	95
Pickles and Vadakams	108
Desserts	111
Snacks	117
Refreshments	138
Cakes and Puddings	141

INDEX

Achchu Murukku	118
Adai	119
Ash Plantain Chips	67
Ash Plantain Curry	66
Ash Plantain Fried	66
Ash Plantain Sambal	96
Ash Pumpkin Curry	67
Awal (Pressed Rice)	119
Baked Crab	40
Biscuit Pudding	162
Bitter Gourd Curry	68
Bitter Gourd Sambal	98
Boiled Lady's Fingers	81
Bonda	120
Bone Rasam	61
Bone Soup	17
Bottle Gourd Curry	69
Brain Omelette	59
Bread Fruit Curry	70
Breaded Chicken	58
Brinjal Curry	70
Brinjal Curry (White)	72
Brinjal Dry Curry	69
Brinjal Kulambu	71
Brinjal Omelette	55
Brinjal Sambal	96
Brinjal Sambal II	97
Buriyani	23
Buriyani Powder	35
Butter Cake	145
Butter Icing	146
Candied Peel	156
Carrot Halva	112
Carrot Sambal	98
Chappathi	12
Cheese Cake	155
Chicken Curry	56
Chicken Curry Black	57
Chicken Kulambu	57
Chocolate Cake	145
Chocolate Eclairs	159
Chocolate Fudge Cake	152
Chocolate Icing	146
Chocolate Swiss Roll	153
Coconut Sambal	98
Coffee Icing	146
Coffee Snow	163
Condiment Powder	33
Coriander Sambal	99
Coriander Sambal II	100
Crab Curry	42
Crab Sodhi	40
Crab Varai	42
Crab With Brinjals	41
Cray Fish Varai	52
Cream Buns	158
Crispy Fried Brinjal	72
Cucumber Sambal	100
Cumin Omelette	55
Curd And Treacle	112
Curd Chillies	109
Curd Pachchadi	101
Curd Rice	22
Curd Vadai	137

Custard	112	Fruit Cake II	148
Cuttle Fish Curry	39	Fruit Salad	113
Devilled Prawns	49	Garam Masala	34
Dhal Curry	73	Ghee Rice	25
Dhal Curry II	74	Ginger Pachchadi	102
Dhal Curry III	75	Gram Flour	31
Dhal Rasam	19	Gram Vadai	136
Doughnut	157	Green Chilli Pachchadi	102
Drumstick Curry	75	Green Gram Balls	121
Drumstick Varai	76	Green Gram Dhal Curry	78
Dundee Cake	148	Hoppers	11
Egg Curry	54	Idli	10
Egg Rice	26	Jaffna Curry Powder	32
Egg Sodhi	77	Jaggery Hoppers	11
Egg Hopper	11	Jaggery Rice	3
Eggless Fruit Cake	161	Jaggery Water	138
Fish Curry	43	Jelebi	123
Fish Curry II	45	Kadalai Curry	79
Fish Cutlet	46	Kali	12
Fish Sodhi	43	Karanai Yam Curry	80
Fish Stock	16	Katta Sambal	103
Fragrant Powder	33	Kesari	114
Fried Bitter Gourd	68	King Yam	108
Fried Brinjal	72	Kolukattai	122
Fried Chicken	58	Kool	18
Fried Cuttle Fish	39	Laddu	124
Fried Fish	44	Lady's Finger Curry	81
Fried Fish Roe	44	Lady's Finger Kulambu	81
Fried Jak Seeds	76	Leeks Varai	78
Fried Lady's Fingers	82	Lemon Cake	145
Fried Liver	61	Lemon Pudding	149
Fried Mutton	60	Lemon Icing	146
Fried Potatoes	84	Lime Pickle	108
Fried Prawns	48	Liver Curry	62
Fried Rice	27	Long Beans Curry	82
Fried Shark	52	Masala Thosai	9
Fruit Cake	145	Milk Hoppers	11

Milk Pittu	8
Milk Rice	2
Milk Rotti	125
Mint Sambal	103
Mixture	126
Mocha Hazelnut Gateau	154
Morr	138
Mothakam	127
Murukku	127
Murunga Leaves Varai	82
Mushroom Omelette	55
Mutton Curry	58
Mutton Kulambu	59
Mutton Stew	60
Mysore Paku	124
Omappodi	128
Omelette	55
Orange Cake	145
Orange Cheese Cake	156
Orange Icing	146
Pagoda	130
Palmyrah Odiyal Laddu	129
Palmyrah Sweet Meat	129
Palmyrah Yam Laddu	128
Payasam	114
Pepper Omelette	55
Peppermint Icing	146
Pineapple Cream	160
Pineapple Pudding	160
Pittu	6
Plain Rice	22
Plantain Dry Curry	67
Plantain Flower Curry	84
Plantain Flower Vadaham	108
Plantain Flower Varai	85
Point Pedro Vadai	131
Poori	8
Porima	130
Pork Curry	63
Pork Smore	62
Potato Curry	83
Potato Sodhi	77
Potato Kulambu	83
Potato Omelette	55
Prawn Curry	47
Prawn Cutlets	50
Prawn Varai	48
Prawn With Drumsticks	50
Rasam	17
Rasawalli Pudding (King Yam)	115
Rice Flour (Roasted)	30
Rice Porridge	2
Rich Cake	150
Ridge Gourd Curry	89
Roasted Black Gram Flour	31
Roasted Green Gram Dhal	31
Roasted Green Gram Flour	31
Roasted Wheat Flour	31
Rum Icing	146
Sambar	86
Sambar Powder	34
Savoury Stringhopper (Vegetable)	6
Seeni Ariyathiram	132
Seeni Sambal	104
Semiya Payasam	115
Semolina Idli	10

Semolina Thosai	9	Tomato Curry	92
Sesame Balls	133	Tomato Sodhi	77
Shark Curry	51	Tomato Kulambu	93
Shark Varai	52	Tomato Sambal	106
Sippi	134	Ulundu Vadai (Black Gram)	136
Snake Gourd Curry	88	Uppuma	13
Snake Gourd Curry II	88	Uurrukai Water	139
Snake Gourd Varai	87	Vadaham	110
Sodhi	77	Valarai Sambal	107
Sour Porridge (Pulic Canji)	20	Vegetable Stock	16
Spicy Chutney Powder	35	Venthayak Kulambu	94
Spinach Curry	90	Woodapple Cream	116
Sponge Cake	147	Yogurt Whip	116
Spring Onion Varai	90	Young Coconut Water	140
Steamed Eggs	54	Young Palmyrah Fruit	140
Steamed Flour	30		
Steamed Flour Pittu	7		
Stock	16		
Stringhopper	4		
Stringhopper Pilau	5		
Sundal	135		
Sweet And Sour Pork	64		
Sweet Palmyrah Toddy	139		
Sweet Pumpkin Curry	91		
Sweet Pumpkin Sambal	105		
Swiss Roll	153		
Tamarind Rice (Pulich Chaadham)	24		
Tapioca Chips	92		
Tapioca Curry	92		
Thosai	9		
Thuthuwalai Sambal	105		
Tinned Fish Curry	46		
Tomato Chutney	106		

Conversion Tables

*These are approximate conversions.
*Never mix metric and imperial measures in one recipe.
*All spoon measurements used in this book are level unless specified otherwise.

Weight

½ oz	15g
¾ oz	20g
1 oz	30g
2 oz	50g
5 oz	150g
10 oz	275g
1 lb	450g
1½ lb	700g
2 lb	900g
3 lb	1.3 kg

1 cup sugar	250g
1 cup flour	225g
1 cup butter	250g

Volume

1 fl oz	28 ml
2	55 ml
3	75 ml
5	150 ml
10	275 ml
15	425 ml
1 pt	570 ml
2 pt	1.2 l
4 pt	2.25 l

¼ cup	60 ml
½ cup	125 ml
1 cup	250 ml
1 tsp	5 ml
1 tbsp	15 ml
1 fl oz	2 tbsp

tbsp:	tablespoonful
tsp:	teaspoonful

Length

¼ inch	½ cm
½ inch	1 cm
¾ inch	2 cm
1 inch	2.5 cm
2 inch	5 cm
4 inch	10 cm
5 inch	13 cm

COOKING TERMS

batter : Flour blended with eggs, water or other liquids such as milk.

blanch : To remove the skin or whiten the ingredients. Steep the ingredients in boiling water and then plunge in cold water.

blend : To mix two or more ingrediants.

cream : Beat the fat and other ingredients into a smooth paste.

deep fry : Cook by completely immersing food in oil or hot fat in a deep pan.

dice : Cut into cubes or squares.

dredge : Sprinkle with flour, sugar or other powder.

dry roast : To cook in a dry hot pan stirring constantly without any liquid or fat.

dust : Sprinkle lightly with sugar, flour or both.

flake : Break into thin small pieces.

fold in : Add another ingredient to a beaten ingredient by blending lightly without loss of air.

knead : Mix the dough by drawing out and pressing with the hands.

marinate : Steep meat and other foods in seasoned sauce or spice before cooking.

preheat : Heat the oven to spcified temperature before placing the food in it.

puree : Make fruits and vegetables into a paste by squeezing them through a sieve.

saute : Fry lightly on top of the stove in a small amount of fat stirring frequently.

shred : Cut into thin match stick like strips.

sift : shake through a sieve.

simmer : Boil gently in liquid over a slow fire.

steam : Cook food by placing above boiling water in a tightly covered perforated pan.

stew : Cook slowly in liquid for a long time until tender.

stir fry : Cooking food in a little hot oil stirring constantly for a short time.

stock : The liquor(liquid) obtained by boiling meat, fish or vegetables.

temper : Fry in hot oil and season.

whip: Beat up eggs, cream or others quickly and throughly until frothy.

SUBSTITUTES

almonds :	cadju nuts and almond essence
capsicum :	red or green pepper
coconut milk :	use coconut cream or powder or any other unsweetened milk
curry leaves :	little bay leaf
evaparated milk :	sterilized milk boiled down to half
fresh scraped coconut :	dessicated coconut soaked in hot water
jaggery :	dark brown moist sugar
lemon grass :	a pinch of lemon rind
maldive fish :	dried prawns or dried crab meat
onions :	white part of leeks
self raising flour :	2 level tsp baking powder for every 4 oz of plain flour.
stock :	ready made cubes
yoghurt :	fresh curd

EQUIVALENT TERMS IN SINHALA AND TAMIL

(For English words for which the Sinhala and Tamil equivalents are commonly used.)

ENGLISH	SINHALA	TAMIL
Asafoetida	Perunkayam	Perunkayam
Atta flour	Thirungu pitti	Atta ma
Black gram	Undu	Ulundu
Caraway	Karum	Seerakam
Cardomom	Enusal	Elam
Celery	Salthiri	Selery
Chick peas	Kadalai	Kadalai
Cloves	Karampunetti	Karampu
Cray Fish	Madu malu	Thirukai
Fenugreek	Ulu hal	Venthayam
Gravy	Hodda(thick)	Kulambu
King yam	Raja ala	Rasavalli
Lady's Finger	Bandakka	Vendikai
Lemon grass	Sera	Sera
Mint leaves	Minchi	Puthina
Mustard	Aba	Kaduhu
Nutmeg	Sadhikai	Sathikai
Ridge gourd	Vatakolu	Pihitkankai
Semolina	Rulang	Ravai
Sesame	Thala	Ellu
Snake gourd	Pathola	Pudalankai
Sweet cumin	Maaduru	Perum seerakam
Toor dhal	Thuvaram parippu	Thuvaram paruppu
Turmeric	Kaha	Manchal
White cumin	Suduru	Nat seerakam
	Katuwal Battu	Thuthuvalai
	Karanai	Karanai yam
	Gotukola	Vallarai
	Mallung	Varai

Jaggery Rice - pongal - prepared for auspicious occasions such as Thai Pongal and New Year.

Thosai with fish curry, dhal and coconut sambal

Idli with sambar, sambal and chutney powder

A Jaffna meal - rice, mutton curry, fried fish, bone rasam, white brinjal curry, tomato kulambu, dhal cuury and vallarai sambal

Kool Ingredients - Prawns, crabs, cray fish, fish, cuttle fish, manioc, long beans, jak seeds, rice, tamarind, chilli powder and palmyrah yam powder.

Kool - the unique rich flavour is produced by the variety of sea food and palmyrah yam powder.

Rasavalli pudding

Snacks and Sweetmeats - vadai, murukku, green gram balls, seeni ariyatharam, jelebi, kolukattai, sippi, mothakam with milk rotti in the centre

BREAKFAST

Milk Rice

3 cups raw rice
2 cups thick coconut milk
6 cups water
salt to taste

Method

1. Wash and destone the rice if required.
2. Place the rice and water in a pan and cook until all the water has been absorbed. If the rice is not soft, add a little hot water and cook until the rice is soft.
3. Add the coconut milk and salt. Stir well, cover and simmer gently for five minutes.
4. After the rice is cooked, remove from the fire and mould the rice into a rice plate. A piece of plantain leaf, buttered paper or even the back of a large spoon could be used to shape the rice. When cold cut into diamond shapes serve with very hot chilli (katta) sambal (page 103).

Rice Porridge

2 cups raw rice
3 cups coconut milk
4 cups water
salt to taste

Method

1. Wash and destone the rice if required. Place the rice and water in a pan and boil until the rice is soft.
2. Add the coconut milk and salt. Mix well and boil for a minute.

Jaggery Rice

250g raw red rice
50g roasted green gram dhal
3 cups water
2 cups thick coconut milk
250g jaggery
100g sugar candy (optional)

50g ghee or butter
50g chopped cadju
50g plums
10 ground cardamom
2 tbsp of honey
(optional)

Method

1. Dissolve the jaggery in the coconut milk.

2. Sauté the cadju and plums in ghee separately and set aside.

3. Wash and destone the rice if required. Place the rice, dhal and water in a pan and cook until all the water has been absorbed. If the rice is not soft add a little hot water and cook until it is soft.

4. Add the jaggery mixture, sugar candy, sautéed cadju and plums, cardamom and honey into the cooked rice and mix well. Simmer for five minutes.

5. Coat an ice cream cup or similar with milk or butter and then press the rice lightly into it. Turn the moulded rice out of the cup on to a serving plate, garnish with the cadju and serve.

Stringhoppers

2 cups roasted or steamed flour   boiling water
salt to taste

Method

1. Sieve the flour into a pan. Add the salt and boiling water. Mix with the handle of a wooden ladle till the mixture is pliable.
2. Fill the stringhopper mould with this mixture and squeeze the mixture on to the stringhopper mats in a circular motion ensuring that the whole of the mat is covered.
3. Place the mats in a steamer and steam for about 7 minutes until the stringhoppers are cooked. While these are steaming press more stringhoppers and have them ready for steaming. This should be a continuous process.

Variations: Stringhoppers can also be made with well steamed wheat flour. However when using wheat flour hot water should be used instead of the boiling water. Kurakkan flour could also be used instead of the wheat flour.

Hints: If the stringhoppers turn out to be hard it is likely that there was too much water in the mixture.
If squeezing the mixture through the mould is difficult try adding a bit more hot water to the mixture.

Stringhopper Pilau

25 string hoppers
250g chicken or any other meat
25g sliced onion
25g capsicum chillies
5 cm rampa
5 cm lemon grass
pepper and salt to taste

10 cardamom (powdered)
25g cadju (chopped)
25g sultanas
6 tbsp soya sauce
4 tbsp oil
3 hard boiled eggs

Preparation

1. Chop the meat into small pieces and season.
2. Break the stringhoppers into small pieces.
3. Chop the capsicum chillies (not too small).
4. Shell and cut the boiled eggs into quarters.

Method

1. Fry the cadju and sultanas separately in a small amount of oil. Remove and keep aside.
2. Using the rest of the oil fry the onions, capsicums, rampa and lemon grass until the onions are golden brown. Add the meat and fry for a further five minutes or until it is cooked.
3. Reduce the heat and add the stringhoppers and cardamom. Mix well and fry for 5 more minutes. Keep turning the mixture continuously to prevent it sticking to the bottom of the pan.
4. Remove from the cooker and immediately mix in the soya sauce and the previously prepared cadju and sultanas. Add salt and pepper to taste.

Savoury Stringhoppers (Vegetable)

As in stringhopper pilau.
Instead of meat use mixed vegetables.
Substitute the eggs with 2 or 3 potatoes.

Method

1. Make as in stringhopper pilau, substituting the meat with mixed vegetables.
2. Cut the potatoes into thin strips and deep fry until golden brown in colour. Keep a close eye on the potatoes as it tends to overcook very easily.
3. Garnish the pilau with these instead of the eggs.

Pittu

2 cups roasted rice flour   1 cup water (cold)
1 cup scraped coconut   salt to taste

Method

1. Put the flour into a pan. Add water and salt and mix in a circular motion using your hands. If the dough is too dry add a bit more water and mix. When mixed thoroughly break the dough into small nodules and flakes.
2. Add the scraped coconut and mix thoroughly making sure that the nodules and flakes don't join together.

3. Fill a special pittu steamer or an ordinary steamer with the mix and steam. As the steam starts to come out at the top, cover and steam for one more minute. If using an ordinary steamer, make some holes in the dough to allow the steam to pass through.

4. Remove from the steamer and serve on a flat plate.

Variation: Lumps left over when rice flour is made (see page 27) can also be used to make pittu. Simply mix the lumps with cold water to a thick consistency and leave to soak for 30 minutes. The mix should now be stiff enough to break into nodules and flakes. If not, add fine flour to make the dough stiffer.

Steamed Flour Pittu

500g flour
(wheat, rice, atta or kurakan)
salt to taste

1 cup hot water
1 cup scraped coconut

Method

1. Thoroughly steam the flour and sieve it.
2. Place the flour and salt in large bowl. Adding a little hot water at a time mix the flour into a dough using the handle of a wooden spoon. Add more hot water if the mix is too dry.
3. Once the dough is mixed well, break into small nodules and flakes. Add the scraped coconut and mix.
4. Steam in the same way as for pittu.

Milk Pittu

4 cups pittu   1 cup thick coconut milk
2 tbsp sugar

Method

1. Using a large bowl dissolve the sugar in the coconut milk.

2. Add the pittu straight from the steamer (i.e. hot) to the milk, cover and leave for five minutes and then serve immediately.

Poori

250g atta flour   100g ghee or butter
water as required   salt to taste
oil for deep frying

Preparation

1. Mix the flour, ghee and salt in a bowl. Add sufficient cold water and mix the flour into a soft dough.

2. Knead well and leave it standing for about one hour.

Method

1. Roll out the dough and cut into thin 10 cm diameter circles.

2. Heat the oil until it is hot before sliding the dough circles into the oil. The dough may puff up. Fry for a minute, turn over and fry until it is golden brown in colour.

Thosai

1 cup black gram dhal
½ cup samba rice
4 onions, (sliced)
1 sprig curry leaves
¼ tsp mustard
salt to taste

1 ½ cups raw rice
2 tsp fenugreek
3 dry chillies (broken)
¼ cummin
1 tbsp oil

Preparation
1. Soak the dhal, rice and fenugreek separately for a minimum of six hours. Wash, drain and then mix the fenugreek and dhal together.
2. Grind the fenugreek/dhal and rice separately into a fine paste adding water as necessary. The paste should flow but not be runny. Mix the two pastes, add salt and leave to ferment overnight (10 hours or longer during cold weather)

Method
1. Temper the onions, chillies and the curry leaves until the onions are golden brown. Add the cumin and mustard and fry for one more minute. Add to the fermented batter and mix well.
2. Heat the griddle and smear it with oil. As soon as the griddle is hot, spread a ladle full of the batter thinly on the griddle. This is best done by pouring the ladle full of batter onto the griddle and then using the underside of the ladle to spread the batter thinly.
3. When the underside is done turn over and cook. Serve hot.

Variations:
Semolina Thosai - Make as Thosai but replace the rice with the same amount of steamed semolina.
Masala Thosai - Make as Thosai but before turning over during cooking spread a spoon of potato curry on the thosai and fold it into two. Cook for half a minute and serve.

Idli

1 cup black gram dhal
½ cup raw rice
salt to taste

3 cups samba rice
2 cups water

Preparation

1. Soak the rice and dhal separately for six hours.
2. Wash, drain and grind separately. The dhal should be ground to a thick and fine paste whereas the rice should be ground to a slightly coarse thick paste.
3. Mix the two pastes together, add the salt and leave to ferment overnight or 8-10 hours.

Method

1. Stir the fermented paste thoroughly. Lightly oil the idli moulds, spoon the paste into them and steam in a steamer or pressure cooker (without weights) for about 7-10 minutes.
2. Remove from the moulds and serve immediately.

Variation:
Semolina Idli - Make as above but replace the rice with the same amount of well steamed semolina.

Hoppers

3 cups raw rice
4 slices bread
1 tbsp sugar

1 cup scraped coconut
2 cups coconut water
or water

Preparation
1. Soak the rice for six hours.
2. Dissolve the sugar in coconut water and soak the bread in it for 15 minutes.
3. Using an electric blender grind the rice and coconut together with water to a smooth paste. Do the same for the soaked bread and water. Mix the two pastes, add the salt and leave to ferment overnight. The paste should flow but not be runny.

Method

1. Heat a thaachi and lightly coat with oil.
2. Stir the batter well and then spoon a small ladle full of the fermented batter into the thaachi. Lifting the thaachi with both hands give it a twist to spread the batter to the sides of the thaachi. Cover tightly and cook until the side of the hopper is crisp.
3. Serve hot with sambal or a meat curry.

Variations:
Egg Hoppers: Cook as hoppers, however before you finally cover, break an egg into the hopper. Cook until the egg is done.

Milk Hoppers: Cook as hoppers, however before you finally cover add 2 table spoons of sweetened thick coconut milk onto the hopper.

Jaggery Hoppers: Cook as hoppers, however before you finally cover add scraped jaggery to the hopper.

Chappathi

250g atta flour   water
salt to taste

Preparation

1. Sieve the flour into a bowl and mix in the salt. Mix the flour into a firm dough adding a little cold water at a time . Knead the dough well and make into one big ball. Cover with damp cloth and leave for an hour or longer.

Method

1. Split the dough into small lime size balls and flatten them out into discs 3 mm thick and 15 cm in diameter.
2. Cook them on a hot iron griddle turning them over to ensure that both sides are cooked.

Kali

2 cups roasted rice flour   or   3 cups raw rice flour
1 cup roasted black gram flour   100g sugar or palmyrah
3 cups coconut milk   jaggery
salt to taste

Method

1. Mix the coconut milk, sugar (or jaggery) and the salt in a heavy pan. Boil for 3 minutes until the jaggery has fully dissolved.

2. Mix both flours thoroughly and add a little of this at a time into the coconut milk stirring continuously with the handle of a wooden spoon.

3. Once all the flour has been added, cover and leave on a low flame for five minutes. Turn the heat off and turn the mixture upside down in the pan to allow the topside to cook in the retained heat.

Uppu Ma

2 cups semolina (slightly roasted)
2 dry chillies
4 red onions
few curry leaves
½ tsp mustard
salt to taste

3 cm piece of ginger
2 tbsp oil
1 cup mixed vegetables
1 cup boiling water
2 tbsp tomato sauce
(optional)

Method

1. Chop the chillies, onions, ginger and the mixed vegetables.

2. Heat the oil in a pan and fry the mustard, chillies, onions and curry leaves for 3 minutes or until the onions are golden brown. Add the vegetables, ginger and salt and fry for a further minute.

3. Add boiling water, cook for a minute and reduce heat. Stir in the semolina a little at a time using the handle of a wooden spoon. As soon as all the semolina has been mixed in, cover and cook for a minute.

4. The tomato sauce could be added to the semolina, if preferred.

Suggested Accompaniments

Jaggery Rice,
Milk Pittu, Kali - Plantains, specially kolikuttu (kappal).

Stringhoppers - Sambal, sambar or dhal curry, potato kulambu, sodhi, any seafood curry, meat curry. (Two would suffice).

Pittu - Sambal, fried brinjal, potato kulambu, tomato kulambu, drumstick curry, fried prawns, omelette, fish curry, meat curry. (Select any suitable three).

Poori - Potato curry, meat curry.

Thosai - Sambal, sambar, or dhall curry, fish curry, meat curry. (A sambal and one curry ould suffice).

Idli - Sambar, pachchadi, tomato chutney, spicy chutney powder.

Chappathi - Potato curry, meat curry.

Uppuma - Seeni sambal, any dry curry, fried potatoes.

SOUPS

Stock

1 kg chicken parts (leftovers, skin, bones, wings etc.)
6 cups water
1 tbsp crushed ginger
1 onion (halved)
Salt to taste
1 tsp pepper
2 whole celery
5 coriander stalks
2 carrots

Method

1. Put all the ingredients in a pan and bring to boil.
2. Simmer for one and a half hours without boiling. Remove from the heat and strain as soon as possible.
3. To reduce the fat content of the stock place, it in a refrigerator to allow the fat to solidify on top of the stock.
4. Once the fat has solidified, skim it off.

Variations:

Fish Stock: Instead of the chicken parts use fish leftovers. e.g. head, small fish and bones.

Vegetable Stock: Use vegetables instead of the chicken parts. Any vegetable could be used. Yams should be avoided.

Rasam

3 tbsp coriander
1 tsp white cumin
1 pod garlic
4 cups water
1 tsp pepper
1 dry chilli
tamarind (marble size)
salt to taste

Method

1. Crush the coriander, pepper, white cumin, chilli and garlic and mix together.

2. Place this mixture in a pan together with the water, tamarind and salt and bring to boil. As soon as it boils, remove from the fire and serve.

Bone Soup

500g bones
5 onions
1 tsp coriander
1 tsp white cumin
6 cups water
1 pod garlic
½ tsp pepper
salt to taste

Method

1. Chop and place the bones in a pan, add the water, onions and salt. Bring to boil and simmer for 30 minutes.

2. Crush and bundle the coriander, pepper, white cumin and the garlic in a cotton cloth.

3. Place the bundled condiments in the pan and simmer for a further 20 minutes to allow the condiments to flavour the broth.

4. Remove the bundled condiments, strain the soup and serve hot.

Kool

150g fish
150g cuttle fish
150g prawns
100g jak seeds
100g spinach
¼ cup palmyrah root flour
10 dry chillies (powdered)
1 ball tamarind (lime size)

150g crabs
150g cray fish
100g long beans
100g tapioca
3 tbsp rice
½ tsp turmeric powder
3 botts water
salt to taste

Preparation

1. Clean and wash the fish and the cuttle fish. Cut the cuttle fish into 3 cm pieces and the fish into larger pieces.
2. Shell the prawns.
3. Wash and quarter the crabs.
4. Clean the cray fish and cut into chunky pieces.
5. Break the beans into 3 cm pieces.
6. Peel and dice the tapioca.
7. Wash and chop the spinach.
8. Cut the jak seeds into halves and then peel off the skin.
9. Soak the flour in a pint of water for ten minutes and then strain the water off.
10. Dissolve the tamarind in one cup of water. Strain and retain the water.

Method

1. Half fill a large pan with water and bring to boil.
2. Add the fish, cuttle fish, prawns, cray fish, crabs, rice, beans, tapioca, jak seeds and salt and cook for about 45 minutes until everything is cooked. Mix in the spinach at this stage.

3. In a separate bowl mix the palmayrah root flour, tamarind solution, chilli powder and turmeric into a thick paste.

4. Add this paste to the seafood broth, mix well and simmer until it thickens. Remove from the fire as soon as the preferred consistency is reached.

Sour Porridge (Pulic Canji)

½ cup coriander
2 tbsp white cumin
¼ tsp turmeric powder
¼ coconut (scraped)
500g prawns
2 cups murunga leaves
50g tamarind

50g garlic
1 tsp pepper
5 dry chillies
¼ cup rice
200g sprats
3 bottles water
salt to taste

Preparation

1. Shell and clean the prawns.
2. Wash the sprats and murunga leaves thoroughly.
3. Dissolve the tamarind in ½ cup of water and strain.
4. Grind the coriander, garlic, white cumin, pepper, turmeric, dry chillies and coconut with water to a smooth paste.

Method

1. Place the rice, prawns, sprats, murunga leaves and salt in a large pan. Add the water and boil for about 30 minutes until the rice becomes soft.
2. Once the rice is cooked, dissolve the condiments paste in a cup of water and add to the cooked mixture.
3. Add the tamarind juice, bring to boil and simmer for 3 minutes. Remove from fire and serve hot.

Dhal Rasam

1 cup toor dhal
2 dry chillies
1 small pod garlic
8 cups water
½ tsp turmeric powder
salt to taste

1 tsp coriander
½ tsp pepper
½ tsp white cumin
marble sized tamarind
2 tomatoes

For Tempering
4 onions (sliced)
1 sprig curry leaves
½ tsp sweet cumin

1 dry chilli (chopped)
½ tsp mustard
2 tsp oil

Preparation

1. Wash and then soak the dhal in 4 cups of water for about an hour.
2. Dissolve the tamarind in a small amount of water and strain.

Method

1. Place the soaked dhal including the water used for soaking in a pan and boil until the dhal is soft. Add more water if required and mash .
2. Dry roast the chillies, coriander, pepper and cumin. Grind them into a fine powder.
3. Boil the tamarind juice, crushed garlic, tomatoes and the ground powder in 4 cups of water for 5 minutes. Add the mashed dhal and simmer for 5 more minutes.
5. Using a separate frying pan temper the onions, curry leaves and chilli for two minutes in hot oil. Add sweet cumin and mustard and temper for a further minute.
4. Remove from the fire and add the tempered ingredients to the dhal water, mix well and serve.

RICE RECIPES

Plain Rice

2 cups samba rice
1 pinch salt
1 tbsp butter

4 cups water
5 cm rampa
5 cm cinnamon

Method

1. Wash and destone the rice if required.
2. Place all the ingredients in a pan and bring to boil. After a minute of boiling, reduce the heat and cook until the rice is soft and all the water has been absorbed.

Curd Rice

6 cups cooked and mashed rice
½ cup milk
½ tsp mustard seeds
2 dry chillies
2 tbsp oil

4 cups curd (fresh if possible)
3 green chillies
1 tsp chopped ginger
1 sprig curry leaves
salt to taste

Method

1. Heat the oil in a frying pan and temper the mustard, dry chillies, ginger, green chillies and curry leaves.
2. Turn this fried mix into the cooked mashed rice.
3. Add salt to the curd and beat it. Mix the curd followed by the milk into the rice.
4. Serve cold.

Buriyani

3 cups rice (basmati or long grain)
4 tbsp oil
200g potatoes
200g tomato
7 green chillies
2 tbsp buriyani masala
mint leaves (few)
salt to taste

750g mutton
100g yoghurt
100g onions
10g ginger
1 pod garlic
coriander leaves (few)
9 cups water

Preparation

1. Prepare the buriyani powder as described on page 35
2. Wash and stone the rice if required.
3. Cut the meat into bite size pieces.
4. Chop the vegetables, onions, green chillies, coriander leaves and the mint leaves.
5. Crush the garlic and ginger.

Method

1. Place 8 cups of water and add the rice in a pan, bring to the boil, cook for 10 minutes and drain off the excess water.
2. While the rice is cooking use a separate heavy bottomed sauce pan to fry the onions until they are crisp and brown. Now add the buriyani powder (mixed in a little water), curd, meat, vegetables, ginger, garlic and the leaves and sauté for two minutes.
3. Add a cup of water to the meat mix and cook on a low flame for 2 minutes before adding the drained rice.
4. Cover and cook on a very low flame for 15 minutes or until all the liquid has been absorbed. Mix well and serve hot.

Tamarind Rice
(Pulich Chaadham)

6 cups cooked rice
6 dry chillies
1 tsp mustard
1 tsp black gram dhal
1 tsp turmeric powder
marble sized tamarind
salt to taste

2 tsp coriander
2 sprigs curry leaves
½ tsp sweet cumin
2 tsp gram dhal
1 pinch asafoetida
½ cup vegetable oil

Preparation

1. Dissolve the tamarind in a cup of water and strain.
2. Roast 2 dry chillies, coriander and black gram dhal. Grind the mix to a coarse powder.
3. Break 4 dry chillies into small pieces.

Method

1. Put the rice in a mixing bowl and set aside.
2. Fry the gram dhal in 2 table spoons of oil until it is golden brown. Add the curry leaves and fry for 30 seconds.
3. Sprinkle this and the previously prepared spice powder onto the rice.
4. Fry the mustard seeds, broken chillies (4 no.), sweet cumin and the asafoetida, in 2 table spoons of oil for 2 minutes. Add the turmeric powder and tamarind juice and cook until the mixture thickens.
5. Add this tamarind mix to the rice and mix well.
6. Heat the remaining oil, pour over the rice and mix well without mashing the rice
7. Serve immediately.

Ghee Rice

2 cups rice
6 red onions (sliced)
½ tsp pepper
10 cardamom
5 cm rampa
50g ghee or butter

4 cups vegetable stock or coconut milk
10 cloves
5 cm cinnamon
5 cm lemon grass

Method

1. Destone and wash the rice if required.
2. Using a pan, fry the onions, rampa, lemon grass, cinnamon, cardamom, and the cloves in ghee until the onions are golden brown in colour. Add the rice and stir fry for a further 2 minutes.
3. Pour stock into the pan, bring to boil and boil for a minute. Reduce to low heat, cover and cook for about 15-20 minutes until all the liquid is absorbed. The rice should be soft. If not add more hot water and cook until it is absorbed.
4. Remove as many of the spices as possible and serve hot.

Egg Rice

2 cups rice
2 eggs
50g margarine
6 cloves
1 tbsp butter

4 cups stock or water
20g red onions (sliced)
¼ tsp pepper corns
5 cm cinnamon
salt and pepper to taste

Method

1. Wash and destone the rice if required.
2. Place the rice, stock or water, pepper corns, cloves, cinnamon and the butter, in a pan and bring to boil. Reduce heat to simmer and cook until all the liquid is absorbed. If the rice is not soft add a little more hot stock or water and cook until it is absorbed.
3. Beat the eggs with salt and pepper.
4. Heat the margarine in a pan and stir fry the sliced onions for 3 minutes. Add the beaten eggs, stir briskly and cook for a further minute.
5. Add the cooked rice to the egg mixture, mix well and serve hot.

Fried Rice

2 cups rice (basmati or samba)

100g cooked prawns
50g green peas
1 leek (sliced)
3 cm piece ginger (crushed)
4 tbsp oil

4 cups chicken stock or water
50g cooked ham or meat
1 carrot (grated)
3 cloves garlic
2 tbsp soy sauce

Method

1. Wash and destone the rice if required.
2. Bring the stock or water to boil in a pan and allow it to simmer.
3. Using a separate pan, fry the rice in hot oil for five minutes or until it is pale. Add the garlic and ginger, stir well and pour into the simmering stock or water.
4. Cover and cook for 20 minutes stirring occasionally.
5. Fold in the leek and carrot and cook for a further 2 minutes before adding the rest of the ingredients. Cook for a further 2 minutes stirring occasionally.

FLOUR & CURRY POWDERS

Rice Flour (Roasted)

Most grocery stores sell rice flour in packets. Flour sold in this way is generally not roasted and therefore needs to be roasted as described below. If you wish to make your own rice flour follow this recipe.

1. Soak the rice for 2-4 hours.
2. Wash, drain and pound or grind the rice.
3. Sieve flour and regrind the retained particles. Repeat until most of the particles are powdered.
4. Dry roast the flour in a large 'Thaachi' stirring continuously until it is dry and flows freely.
5. Once roasted sieve the flour and save the lumps to make pittu (see pittu recipe). Store the fine flour in an airtight container. The flour if it had been roasted until it is completely dry will keep for months.

Hint: Too much flour in the thaachi will make it difficult to move the flour around continuously and may result in the flour sticking at the bottom and getting burnt.

Steamed Rice Flour

Sift the flour and pack it in paper or a piece of cloth. Place the package in a steamer, cover and steam until it becomes firm to the touch. Remove from the steamer, break up the flour and sieve. This flour can be used to make pittu, stringhopper etc.

Steam wheat flour, atta flour, kurakkan flour and semolina as above.

Roasted Wheat Flour

Sieve the flour and roast as for rice flour but on a low flame. Store in an airtight container. This flour is used to make pittu.

Roasted Green Gram Dhal

Wash and destone the green gram.

Dry roast in a thaachi ensuring that the gram is moved around continuously. When the grams start to pop and the fragrance comes out remove from the fire.

Allow to cool and lightly pound in a mortar or crush lightly under a rolling pin. Winnow to remove husk and skin. Repeat if neccessary to remove the skin from all the grains. The dhal should be a golden colour.

Roasted Green Gram Flour: Grind the roasted green gram dhal in to a fine powder. Sieve before use.

Roasted Black Gram Flour: Prepare as roasted green gram flour using black gram.

Gram Flour

Gram flour is freely available in grocery stores. If you wish to make your own, clean the dhal and grind it in to a fine powder. Sieve before use.

CURRY POWDERS

Jaffna Curry Powder (Hot)

500g dry chillies
100g pepper
200g white cumin
10 cm turmeric

500g coriander
100g sweet cumin
50g fenugreek (optional)
3-4 sprigs curry leaves

Method

1. Clean and break the chillies into large pieces.

2. Place the chillies, coriander, pepper, turmeric and curry leaves in a 'Thaachi' and dry roast on a medium fire until the curry leaves are crisp. Remove and set aside. Keep turning the mixture constantly to avoid burning.

3. Mix the sweet cumin, white cumin and fenugreek and dry roast in the 'Thaachi' until the cumin seeds are golden brown in colour.

4. Mix the roasted ingredients together and get the mix ground into a fine powder at a local grinding mills. If preferred the mix could be pounded at home.

5. This powder can be stored for many months in an air tight container.

Variations: If the powder turns out to be too hot, roast 250g-500g of coriander. Grind it and mix with the chilli powder. Alternatively curries could be made milder by substituting some of the chilli powder with the coriander powder.

Condiment Powder

500g coriander 400g white cumin
25g pepper 10g turmeric

Method

1. Clean and dry roast the ingredients in a 'Thaachi' for ten minutes.
2. Get the roasted mix ground into a fine powder at the local grinding mills. Alternatively the mix could be pounded at home.
3. This powder can be stored in an air tight container for many months.

Fragrant Powder

100g sweet cumin 2 tbsp coriander
10g mixed spice 2 tbsp black gram dhal
100g raw rice

Method

1. Dry roast the ingredients in a 'Thaachi' until they are golden brown in colour.
2. Get the roasted mix ground into a fine powder at the local grinding mills. Alternatively the mix could be pounded at home.
3. This powder can be stored in an air tight container for many months.

Garam Masala

100g coriander
25g pepper
50 cloves
25 cm cinnamon sticks

50g white cumin
50 cardamom
¼ nutmeg

Method

1. Break the cinnamon sticks into small pieces.
2. Individually roast each of the ingredients over a low flame until they are golden brown in colour.
3. Once cooled break open the cardamom pods and retrieve the dark seeds from within. Discard the shells.
4. Place all the roasted spices in a clean grinder and grind into a fine powder.
5. This powder can be stored in an air tight container for many months.

Sambar Powder

100g dry chillies
25g pepper
25g toor dhal

100g coriander
25g gram dhal
20g turmeric

Method

1. Clean and dry the ingredients in the hot sun for a day.
2. Mix the ingredients and get it ground into a fine powder at the local grinding mills. Alternatively the mix could be pounded at home.

Spicy Chutney Powder

50g dry chillies
40g gram dhal
1 pinch asafoetida
salt to taste

50g black gram dhal
15g sesame seeds
2 tbsp oil

Method

1. Heat the oil in a pan and fry the dry chillies for 2 minutes on medium heat. Remove the chillies.
2. In the same pan fry the rest of the ingredients over medium heat until golden brown.
3. Mix all the fried ingredients and grind them with salt to a fine powder.

Hint: Mix a spoonful of this powder with half a spoonful of sesame oil and eat with **Thosai or Idly.**

Buriyani Powder

50g coriander
10g cumin seeds
10g pepper
5g cloves

25g red chillies
5g caraway seeds
5g cardamom

Method

1. Mix and dry roast all the ingredients until they are golden brown in colour.
2. Pound the roasted mix into a fine powder or grind in a grinder.

CURRIES

General Notes on Curry Recipes

- The curries, in these recipes are moderately spicy. However they could be made mild by using less curry powder or by omitting the curry powder.
- Unless otherwise specified, coconut milk made up of a combination of thick and thin milk should be used.
- Tamarind measures specified in these recipes are based on using tamarind with seeds. When using tamarind pulp, use lesser quantities.
- Large onions mean Bombay onions. If red onions are not available use Bombay onions.
- Use freshly ground black pepper where pepper is specified.
- Green leaves should be cooked uncovered to retain the colour and flavour.
- Where lime juice is specified let the curry cool a little before adding it.
- If stock is not available, use stock cubes available from the shops.
- Always cook on medium heat unless otherwise stated and fry on both sides.

- **Varai**: Sinhala **Mallung**.
- **Kulambu**: is a thick gravy of flowing consistency made with curry powder.
- **Sodhi**: Sinhala **Hodda**. A thin gravy made with very little spices.

SEA FOODS

Cuttle Fish Curry

500g cuttle fish
2 green chillies [slit]
1 tbsp curry powder

1 tbsp onions [sliced]
1 cup thick coconut milk
salt to taste

Method

1. Wash and cut the cuttle fish into small squares, rings or strips.
2. Place the cuttle fish in a pan with 1 cup of water, onions, chillies and salt, bring to boil and cook for 30 minutes or until all the liquid has evaporated and the cuttle fish is soft.
3. Pour in the coconut milk with the curry powder, bring to boil and simmer for 10 minutes to thicken the gravy.

Fried Cuttle Fish

500g cuttle fish
4 tbsp gingelly oil

1 tsp curry powder
salt to taste

Method

1. Wash the cuttle fish and cut into small squares, rings or strips.
2. Season with curry powder and salt and leave for 10 minutes.
3. Heat the oil in a skillet. Once the oil is hot, place the cuttle fish in it. Cover immediately to prevent the oil splattering.
4. Fry for ten minutes stirring occasionally. Two minutes before removing from the fire add the onions.

Crab Sodhi

500g crabs or claws
4 red onions
4 green chillies
¼ tsp turmeric powder
salt to taste

3 cups thin coconut milk
1 cup thick coconut milk
1 tsp fenugreek
marble sized tamarind

Method

1. Wash and halve the crabs. Discard the main body shell. Break the claws into two.

2. Dissolve the tamarind in the coconut milk and strain.

3. Put all the ingredients in a pan, bring to boil and cook on reduced heat for 15 minutes.

Baked Crab

500g medium sized crabs
2 tbsp tomato sauce
½ tsp curry or pepper powder
cheese bread crumbs

4 onions (chopped)
salt to taste
1 beaten egg or grated

Method

1. Wash and halve the crabs retaining the main body shell separately.

2. Boil the crabs in water for ten minutes and shell them to collect the meat.

3. Add the curry or pepper powder together with onions, tomato sauce and salt to the crab meat and mix well.
4. Place this mixture in the body shell, brush with beaten egg. Sprinkle bread crumbs and a few small pats of butter over it. Grated cheese is an alternative to the egg, bread crumbs and butter.
5. Bake in a moderate oven (350°F/180°C Gas Mark 4) until the bread crumbs are brown or until the cheese has melted and slightly browned.

Crabs With Brinjals

250g crabs
1 tbsp sliced onions
3 green chillies (chopped)
salt to taste

250g brinjals
1 tsp garam masala
2 cups coconut milk

Method

1. Cut the brinjals into 5 cm long thin slices. Soak in water for a minute, remove and squeeze out the water.
2. Wash and halve the crabs discarding the main body shell. Boil the crabs in half a cup of water for ten minutes. When cooked shell and remove the meat.
3. Mix the crab meat and the rest of the ingredients with the brinjals. Bring to boil, reduce heat and cook for about 15-20 minutes until the gravy thickens.

Variation:
Instead of adding crab meat to the brinjals add the raw crab quartered.

Crab Curry

500g crabs
4 red onions (sliced)
4 cloves garlic (sliced)
2 tbsp murunga leaves (opt)
marble sized tamarind

2 cups coconut milk
1 tsp fenugreek
1 tbsp curry powder
salt to taste

Method

1. Wash and halve the crabs. Discard the main body shell. Break the claws into two.
2. Dissolve the tamarind in the coconut milk and strain.
3. Place all the ingredients in a pan bring to boil, reduce heat and cook until the gravy thickens (15-20 min).

Crab Varai

500g crabs
½ cup scraped coconut
2 dry chillies (chopped)
2 tbsp oil

4 red onions (sliced)
1 tsp curry powder
½ tsp white cumin
salt to taste

Method

1. Wash and halve the crabs. Discard the main body shell.
2. Boil the crabs in one cup of water for ten minutes. Drain the water and shell the crabs to extract the meat. Mix the crab meat with the curry powder, salt and coconut.
3. Fry the onions and chillies in the oil until the onions are nicely browned. Add the cumin seed and sauté for a minute.
4. Mix the seasoned crab meat with the onion mixture and stir fry for a about 10-15 minutes until the meat is dry.

Fish Curry

500g fish
2 cloves garlic (sliced)
marble sized tamarind
1 tbsp curry powder

4 red onions (sliced)
2 green chillies (chopped)
3 cups coconut milk
salt to taste

Method

1. Dissolve the tamarind in half a cup of water and strain.
2. Place all the ingredients (including the tamarind water) in a sauce pan, bring to boil, reduce to medium heat and cook for 15 minutes until the gravy thickens.

Fish Sodhi

250g fish, fish head or small fish
4 green chillies
¼ tsp turmeric powder
salt to taste

2 tbsp sliced onions
3 cups coconut milk
marble sized tamarind

Method

1. Wash and clean the fish as required.
2. Dissolve the tamarind in half a cup of water and strain.
3. Place all ingredients (including tamarind water) in a pan, bring to boil and simmer for 15 minutes.

Fried Fish

8 slices fish
4 sliced onions
oil for frying

¼ tsp curry powder
salt to taste

Method

1. Wash the fish and rub in the salt and curry powder. Leave for 15 minutes.
2. Heat the oil in a frying pan, slide the fish into the oil and fry for 5 minutes at medium heat. Turn over and fry for a further 2 minutes. Add the onions and continue frying until the onions are golden brown.
3. Remove from the oil, drain off excess oil and place on absorbent paper to remove any oil left over.

Variations: Instead of the curry powder, a mixture containing equal amounts of turmeric and chilli powder may be used.
As another variation the fish could be seasoned as in 1 above, dipped in beaten egg, coated with bread crumbs and fried until golden brown in colour.
Alternatively rub salt and pepper into the fish, dust with flour and fry as above.

Fried Fish Roe

500g fish roe
¼ tsp turmeric powder
25g bread crumbs
oil for frying

1 tsp chilli powder
1 egg
salt to taste

Method

1. Wash the roe carefully without breaking it. **Cut out any traces of green colour and discard.** If this is not done the roe will be unpalatable.

2. Boil in salted water for 10 minutes and drain.

3. Cut into bite size pieces, season with chilli powder, turmeric powder and salt.

4. Dip in beaten egg, coat with bread crumbs and deep fry in medium heat until golden brown.

Fish Curry II

500g fish
1 tbsp coriander
4 dry chillies
½ tsp turmeric powder
3 cloves garlic (sliced)
salt to taste

3 red onions (sliced)
½ tsp pepper
1 tsp white cumin
25g coconut pieces
marble size tamarind

Method

1. Dissolve the tamarind in one cup of water and strain.

2. Grind the coriander, pepper, chillies, cumin, turmeric and the coconut into a fine paste.

3. Wash the fish and cut into pieces.

4. Place the fish and the tamarind juice in a pan. Add onions, garlic, salt and the paste, dissolved in two cups of water to the fish. Bring to boil and simmer for 15 minutes.

Tinned Fish Curry

1 tin of fish
2 green chillies (chopped)
2 cm ginger
5 cm lemon grass
2 cups coconut milk
1 tbsp oil
salt to taste

2 tbsp sliced onions
2 cloves of garlic
5 cm rampa
1 tsp fenugreek
1 tbsp curry powder
marble sized tamarind

Method

1. Remove the skin and bones from the tin fish.
2. Crush the garlic and ginger.
3. Dissolve the tamarind in half a cup of water and strain.
4. Fry the garlic, ginger, onion, green chillies, rampa and lemon grass in hot oil until the onions are soft.
5. Add the fenugreek, stir fry one minute before adding the tamarind juice, coconut milk, salt and curry powder. Cook for five minutes.
6. Add the fish and cook for a further five minutes.

Fish Cutlet

500g boiled or canned fish
2 tbsp chopped onions
2 eggs (well beaten)
1 sprig curry leaves
½ lime
oil for frying

250g boiled potatoes
4 green chillies, finely chopped
1 tsp pepper powder
salt to taste
100g bread crumbs

Method

1. Skin and bone the fish if required and crumble into small pieces.
2. Peel and mash the potatoes. Mix the fish with the potatoes and then add the salt and pepper.
3. Fry the onions, green chillies and curry leaves until the onions are transparent. Thoroughly mix in the fish mixture and remove from the fire. Add lime juice.
4. Make 3 cm diameter balls of the mixture dip them in the beaten egg and then coat with bread crumbs.
5. Heat sufficient oil in a deep frying pan and deep fry in medium heat until the bread crumbs become golden brown. Serve hot.

Prawn Curry

500g prawns
2 green chillies (chopped)
1 tbsp curry powder
3 cups coconut milk (medium)
5 cm lemon grass
salt to taste

4 red onions (sliced)
2 cloves garlic (sliced)
½ tsp fenugreek
5 cm rampa
marble size tamarind

Method

1. Wash and shell the prawns.
2. Dissolve the tamarind in the coconut milk and strain.
3. Add all the ingredients into a pan and bring to boil, reduce heat and cook for 15 minutes or until the gravy reaches the preferred consistency.

Fried Prawns

500g prawns
3 tbsp sesame oil
salt to taste

½ tsp curry powder
2 tbsp red onions (sliced)

Method

1. Wash and shell the prawns.
2. Season the prawns with the curry powder and salt. Set aside for 10 minutes.
3. Heat the oil in a frying pan and slide the prawns into the hot oil. Fry without stirring for 3 minutes. After this stir frequently and fry for a further 15 minutes.
4. Add the onions and continue frying until the onions are crisp.
5. Remove from the oil draining as much of the oil as possible. Place on absorbent paper to remove the excess oil.

Variation

Season the prawns with salt and pepper. Make a smooth batter using 1 cup flour, 1 cup milk/water, 1 beaten egg, 1 pinch of baking powder and salt to taste. Dip the prawns in this batter and deep fry in vegetable oil to a golden brown colour.

Prawn Varai

500g prawns
3 dry chillies (chopped)
1 cup scraped coconut
2 tbsp oil

10 red onions (sliced)
1 tsp curry powder
salt to taste

Method

1. Clean and shell the prawns, boil and mince them.
2. Mix the curry powder, coconut and salt with the minced prawns.
3. Fry the dry chillies and the onions. When the onions are golden brown in colour add the prawn mixture and mix well.
4. Reduce heat and stir fry the mixture for about 15 minutes until the mixture is dry.

Devilled Prawns

500g prawns
100g capsicum chillies
4 cloves garlic (sliced)
1 tsp chilli powder
2 tbsp vinegar
salt to taste

200g tomatoes
1 large onion (sliced)
3 cm ginger (crushed)
½ tsp pepper powder
2 tbsp oil

Method

1. Wash and shell the prawns.
2. Blanch the tomatoes by placing them in boiling water for 2 minutes. Peel their skin off and puree.
3. Cut the capsicum into 2 cm slices.
4. Heat the oil in a frying pan and stir fry the onions, garlic and ginger until the onions are golden brown in colour.
5. Add the prawns, chilli powder, pepper powder, vinegar and salt and stir fry for a further five minutes.
6. Add the tomato puree and the capsicums and stir fry for five minutes. Remove from the fire and serve hot.

Prawns With Drumsticks

250g prawns
1 tbsp sliced onions
2 cups thick coconut milk
salt to taste

250g drumsticks
2 tsp curry powder
2 cups thin coconut milk

Method

1. Clean and shell the prawns.
2. Cut the drumsticks into 8 cm long pieces. Split them into two and wash them.
3. Place all the ingredients in a pan and boil for 5 minutes. Reduce heat, cover and cook for 15-20 minutes until the gravy thickens.

Prawn Cutlets

500g prawns
50g onions
½ tsp pepper powder
1 sprig curry leaves
1 egg
oil for frying

250g potatoes
3 green chillies
½ lime
salt to taste
50g bread crumbs

Method

1. Boil, peel and mash the potatoes.
2. Wash, shell, boil and mince the prawns.
3. Finely chop the onions, curry leaves and the green chillies.

4. Mix the mashed potatoes, minced prawns, onions, chillies, curry leaves, pepper and salt. Squeeze the lime juice into the mixture and mix well.
5. Form the mixture into 4 cm diameter oblong or round shapes.
6. Beat the egg. Coat the shaped mixture with the beaten egg and roll it in the bread crumbs until it is fully covered with bread crumbs.
7. Deep fry in hot oil until the cutlets are light brown in colour.
8. Serve hot.

Shark Curry

500g shark
1 tbsp onions (sliced)
2 tbsp oil
½ tsp fenugreek
marble sized tamarind
salt to taste

1 cup coconut milk
2 green chillies (slit)
2 tsp curry powder
½ tsp mustard seeds
1 sprig curry leaves

Method

1. Cut the shark meat into 5 cm, cube shaped pieces. Season with curry powder and salt.
2. Dissolve the tamarind in half a cup of water and strain.
3. Fry the onions, chillies and curry leaves in the oil until the onions are brown. Add the fenugreek and mustard, fry for one more minute.
4. Add the shark, stir, cover and cook until all the liquid has evaporated. Pour in the tamarind water and coconut milk, continue cooking until the gravy thickens.

Shark Varai

500g small shark
1 cup scraped coconut
1 tbsp sliced onions
sprig of curry leaves

1 tsp curry powder
2 broken dry chillies
½ tsp white cumin
salt to taste

Method
1. Clean and cut the shark into small pieces. Wash well and boil in a quarter cup of water. Cook until all the liquid has evaporated.
2. Remove the skin and bones from the boiled shark and break up the meat. Mix this in a bowl with the curry powder, salt and the coconut.
3. Fry the onions, chillies and curry leaves in 2 table spoons of oil. As the onion begins to brown add in the cumin and fry for few seconds before adding the shark meat mixture. Stir fry until the mixture is quite dry.

Variation:
Cray Fish Varai-Cook as shark varai replacing the shark with cray fish.

Fried Shark

500g shark
2 tbsp sliced onions
oil for frying

1 tsp curry powder
salt to taste

Method
1. Clean and wash the shark and cut it into 5 cm pieces.
2. Season with salt and curry powder.
3. Deep fry in hot oil until the meat is golden brown all over. Add the onions a few minutes before removing the shark from the oil.
4. Remove the shark and onions from the oil and place on absorbent paper.

EGG
&
MEAT

Egg Curry

4 eggs (hard boiled)
2 green chillies (slit)
½ tsp fenugreek
5 cm each rampa, lemon grass
or 1 sprig curry leaves
¼ tsp. turmeric powder
salt to taste

1 tbsp onions (sliced)
3 cloves garlic (sliced)
¾ tbsp curry powder
marble sized tamarind
2 cups coconut milk
1 tbsp oil

Method

1. Shell the eggs. Prick them with a skewer, rub in the turmeric powder and stir fry in oil until the eggs are golden in colour.
2. Dissolve the tamarind in quarter cup of water and strain.
3. Place all the ingredients except the eggs in a pan, bring to boil and cook for ten minutes.
4. Add the eggs and cook for a further five minutes.

Steamed Eggs

4 eggs
8 green chillies (chopped)

100g onions (sliced)
pepper and salt

Method

1. Beat the eggs well. Thoroughly mix in the rest of the ingredients to the egg.
2. Grease a shallow dish pour in the egg mixture and steam until the top is firm to touch. Serve hot.

Omelette

4 eggs
8 green chillies (chopped)
4 tbsp gingelly oil
100g red onions (sliced)
2 tsp. curry powder
salt to taste

Method

1. Break the eggs into a bowl. Beat well adding curry powder and salt.
2. Heat the oil in a frying pan, fry the onions and chillies until the onions are soft.
3. Add the beaten egg and fry until the top is set. Turn over and fry until golden in colour and serve immediately.

Variations :

Mushroom Omelette: Fry 50g sliced mushroom with onion and make as above.

Potato Omelette : Cut 50g potatoes into small pieces and fry with onions and make as above.

Brinjal Omelette: Cut the brinjal into small pieces, and soak in water for 2 minutes. Squeeze to remove water, and add to the onion.

Pepper Omelette: Add pepper instead of the curry powder to the eggs.

Cumin Omelette: Grind 2 tsp. white cumin and ¼ tsp. turmeric powder and use this instead of the curry powder.

Chicken Curry

1½ kg chicken
4 pips garlic (crushed)
2 cup coconut milk
100g onions (sliced)
1 sprig curry leaves
½ tsp. mustard
2 tbsp oil

1 tbsp curry powder
3 cm piece ginger (crushed)
3 dry chillies (broken)
1 tsp sweet cumin
1 lime
salt to taste

Method

1. Skin, clean and bone the chicken. Cut into small pieces.
2. Season with a tea spoon of curry powder, ginger, garlic and salt. Marinate for twenty minutes.
3. Heat the oil in a pan and fry the onions, dry chillies and curry leaves. When the onions are golden brown mix in the sweet cumin and mustard. Fry for a further minute.
4. Add the chicken, cover and cook on medium heat for five minutes. Uncover, stir, cover and cook for five more minutes. Repeat until most of the liquid has been absorbed.
5. Pour in the coconut milk with the rest of the curry powder. Cook until the gravy has thickened and the chicken is coated with the gravy.
6. Remove from fire and add lime juice.

Chicken Curry Black

Make some white cumin powder by roasting 1 tbsp of white cumin until it is dark brown in colour. Grind it into a fine powder. Cook the chicken as in chicken curry but before finally removing from the fire, add the white cumin powder and mix well.

Chicken Kulambu

1½ kg chicken
100g onions (sliced)
4 cups thick and thin
  coconut milk
1 tbsp curry powder
1 sprig of curry leaves
1 lime

500g potatoes
5 green chillies (slit)
5 cm pieces of rampa &
  lemon grass
2 tsp fragrant powder
1 tbsp oil
salt to taste

Method

1. Skin, clean and cut the chicken into pieces.

2. Peel and cut the potatoes.

3. Fry the onions, green chillies, curry leaves, rampa and lemon grass in a pan until the onions are browned. Stir in the chicken, potatoes and salt. Cover and cook for five minutes.

4. Pour in the coconut milk with the curry powder. Stir, cover and cook till the gravy is thick.

5. Stir in the fragrant powder. Cook for one minute. Remove from the heat and add lime juice.

Fried Chicken

1½ kg chicken
salt to taste
2 tsp curry powder
oil for frying

Method

1. Skin and clean the chicken. Cut into pieces.
2. Season with curry powder and salt. Leave for 15 minutes.
3. Fry in hot oil until the chicken turns to a golden colour. Remember to turn the pieces to allow it to cook evenly.

Variation:
Breaded Chicken: Season 4 tbsp flour with pepper and salt and coat the chicken pieces, then dip in the beaten egg and coat with bread crumbs. Fry until the bread crumbs are golden brown in colour.

Mutton Curry

500g mutton
2 dry chillies, broken
½ tsp mustard seeds
1 tbsp curry powder
1 cup thick coconut milk
salt to taste
1 tbsp onions, sliced
1 sprig curry leaves
½ tsp sweet cumin
1 cup thin coconut milk
1 tbsp oil

Method

1. Cut the mutton into small pieces.
2. Season with curry powder and salt and leave to marinate for 20 to 25 minutes.

3. Heat the oil in a pan, fry the onions, chillies and curry leaves. As soon as the onions are slightly browned add the sweet cumin and the mustard seeds.
4. Sauté for a minute and add the mutton, cover and cook for five minutes. Uncover, stir well, cover and cook until most of the liquid has evaporated.
5. Pour in the coconut milk and simmer until the gravy has thickened and the meat is tender.

Brain Omelette

1 brain (goat)
100g onions, chopped
1 tsp.curry powder
salt to taste

2 eggs
3 green chillies, chopped
4 tbsp oil

Method

1. Mix the brain and the eggs together and beat well. Add in the salt and curry powder and beat well.
2. Using a frying pan fry the onions and chillies in oil until the onions are soft. Pour in the egg mixture spreading it evenly. Cook over a low heat until the surface is set. Turn over and cook until it turns golden in colour.

Mutton Kulambu

Prepare as in chicken kulambu but use 500g mutton instead of chicken

Mutton Stew

500g mutton
2 tbsp butter
150g tomato puree
100g carrot, sliced
1 stick celery, sliced
1 bay leaf

50g onions, sliced
1 ½ cups stock
150g potatoes
100g cabbage, shredded
1 parsley sprig
pepper and salt

Method

1. Clean and wash the mutton. Cut into 4 cm cubes.
2. Peel the potatoes and dice them.
3. In a heavy pan melt the butter and sauté the onions and meat until the onions are soft and lightly browned.
4. Pour in half a cup of stock and then stir in the tomato puree.
5. Add the rest of the ingredients, bring to boil and simmer until the meat is tender. Serve hot.

Fried Mutton

500g boneless mutton
1 tbsp sliced onions
salt to taste

2 tsp curry powder
3 tbsp oil

Method

1. Clean and cut the meat into small pieces.
2. Season with curry powder and salt. Marinate for 20 minutes.
3. Heat the oil and fry until the meat is tender. Mix in the onions and continue frying until the onions are browned.

Bone Rasam

500g bones
1 tsp. pepper
1 pod garlic
½ cup thick coconut milk
1 lime

2 tbsp coriander
½ tsp. white cumin
3 cups thin coconut milk
2 cups water
salt to taste

Method

1. Wash the bones. Place in a pan with water and salt, bring to boil and simmer for 30 minutes.

2. Crush the coriander, pepper, white cumin and garlic.

3. Add the coconut milk and the crushed condiments to the bone mixture. Bring to boil and simmer for 5 minutes.

4. Remove from the fire and add lime juice.

Fried Liver

500g liver
4 tbsp oil
salt to taste

1 tsp. curry powder
2 tbsp onions (sliced)

Method

1. Cut the liver into 3 cm cubes, season with curry powder and salt.

2. Heat the oil in a pan, slide in the liver and fry gently for 15 minutes stirring occasionally.

3. Mix in the onions and continue frying until they are lightly browned.

Liver Curry

500g liver
2 tbsp flour
1 tsp curry powder
200g potatoes
1 sprig curry leaves
2 cups coconut milk

1 tsp ground pepper
100g onions (sliced)
2 cloves garlic (crushed)
200g tomato (sliced)
2 tbsp oil
salt to taste

Method

1. Cut the liver into strips.
2. Peel and dice the potatoes.
3. Mix the flour, salt and pepper and use it to coat the liver strips.
4. Heat the oil in a pan and lightly fry the liver for two minutes on each side. Remove the liver from the pan and keep hot.
5. Fry the onions, garlic and curry leaves in the same pan until the onions are softened. Stir in the potatoes, tomatoes and curry powder and fry for a minute.
6. Pour the coconut milk bring to boil and then add the fried liver, cover and simmer for 20 minutes.

Pork Smore

1 kg pork
4 cloves garlic (chopped)
5 cm piece cinnamon, rampa
5 cm lemon grass
5 tbsp vinegar
2 tbsp margarine
1 cup thick coconut milk
2 tomatoes (quartered)
salt to taste

1 tbsp red onions (sliced)
3 cm ginger (chopped)
1 sprig curry leaves
2 tbsp curry powder
½ lime
3 cloves 3 cardamom
6 cups water
5 capsicums
(cut into 5 cm pieces)

Method

1. Wash and cut the pork into 3 cm pieces, and prick them with a fork or skewer.
2. Put all the ingredients except the coconut milk, tomatoes, capsicums and margarine into a heavy bottom pan and boil gently until the meat is tender.
3. Pour in the coconut milk and cook for 15 minutes longer. Drain and retain the gravy. Fry the meat in the margarine for 3 minutes.
4. Pour the gravy back into the meat with the tomatoes and capsicums. Cook for a few minutes.

Pork Curry

500g pork
3 tbsp onions (sliced)
1 sprig curry leaves
1 tbsp oil

1 tbsp curry powder
3 dry chillies (broken)
1½ cups water
salt to taste

Method

1. Cut the pork into 3 cm cubes and season with salt and curry powder. Marinate for 20 minutes.
2. Fry the onions, chillies and curry leaves in a pan until the onions are browned and then add in the meat. Stir fry for 2 minutes.
3. Cover and cook for 15 minutes. Add water and cook, until the meat is tender and the gravy is thick.

Sweet and Sour Pork

500g lean pork
pepper and salt
3 tbsp flour
1 tbsp oil
½ cup pineapple juice
2 tbsp tomato puree
4 tsp. corn flour
2 spring onions cut into 3 cm pieces
2 green pepper (sliced)

50g plain flour
3 egg yolks
3 tbsp water
500g canned pineapple pieces
6 tbsp malt vinegar
5 tsp. soft brown sugar
3 tbsp water
oil for frying

Method

1. Cut the pork into bite size pieces and coat with a mixture of plain flour, salt and pepper.
2. Beat the egg yolks, flour, salt and water together to make a batter.
3. Dip the pork pieces in the batter and fry them in a pan to a golden brown colour. Drain and place on a serving dish keeping it warm.
4. Drain the pineapple pieces and retain the juice.
5. Put half a cup of juice, vinegar, tomato puree, sugar, corn flour and water into a pan, bring to boil and simmer for 2 minutes stirring continuously.
6. In a separate frying pan fry the spring onion and green pepper in 1 tbsp oil for a minute. Add this to the pineapple juice mixture and mix well.
7. Pour this sauce over the fried pork and serve hot.

VEGETABLES

Ash Plantain Curry

250g ash plantain
2 green chillies (chopped)
3 cups coconut milk
1 sprig of curry leaves
1 tbsp maldive fish (pounded)
      optional

4 red onions (sliced)
1 tsp curry powder
3 dry chillies
½ tsp sweet cumin
salt to taste

Method

1. Skin the plantains and cut into thick slices. Coat the slices with lime juice and wash.
2. Place the plantain slices, onions, chillies, curry powder, curry leaves, coconut milk, salt and if desired the maldive fish in a pan. Bring to boil, stir, cover and cook over medium heat for 15 minutes.
3. Coarsely powder the chillies with the cumin and add it to the curry, mix well and simmer for 5 minutes.

Ash Plantain Fried

250g ash plantain
1 tbsp onions (sliced)
salt to taste

1 tsp curry powder
few curry leaves
oil for frying

Method

1. Peel and cut the plantain into 2 cm cubes and wash them.
2. Season with salt and curry powder before deep frying in hot oil to a crisp and golden colour. Two minutes before removing from the fire add the onions and curry leaves.

Ash Plantain Chips

Cut 250g of ash plantain into thin slices and season with ¼ tsp turmeric powder and salt and deep fry in hot oil until they are crisp.

Plantain Dry Curry

Cook as brinjal dry curry.

Ash Pumpkin Curry

250g ash pumpkin
2 tbsp onions (sliced)
¼ cup thick coconut milk
1 sprig curry leaves
4 green chillies (chopped)
¼ tsp turmeric powder
½ lime
salt to taste

Method

1. Skin and cut the pumpkin into small pieces.
2. Wash and place in a pan along with all other ingredients except lime. Cover and cook over a low fire stirring occasionally.
3. Remove from the fire just before the curry becomes dry and add the lime juice stirring well

Bitter Gourd Curry

250g bitter gourd
2 green chillies (chopped)
1½ cups coconut water
2 cup thick coconut milk
salt to taste

4 red onions (sliced)
marble sized tamarind
3 tsp curry powder
1 tsp sugar

Method

1. Break the bitter gourd into 5 cm pieces, remove the seeds, cut into strips or rings and then wash them.
2. Dissolve the tamarind in the coconut water and strain.
3. Cover and cook the bitter gourd, onions, chillies and tamarind dissolved in coconut water, in a pan, over medium heat until the water is absorbed.
4. Add curry powder, coconut milk and salt, stir and cook on medium heat until the gravy thickens. Mix in the sugar just before taking the curry off the fire.

Fried Bitter Gourd

250g bitter gourd
2 tsp salt
oil for frying

1 tsp curry powder
2 tbsp onions (sliced)

Method

1. Finely slice the bitter gourd and remove the seeds. Season with salt and leave for 10 minutes.
2. Squeeze out the liquid in the bitter gourd and mix with curry powder.

3. Deep fry in hot oil stirring frequently until it turns a golden colour. Two minutes before removing from the fire add the onions. Remove from fire and drain off the excess oil.

Brinjal Dry Curry

250g brinjal
100g onions (sliced)
4 cloves garlic (chopped)
2 tbsp maldive fish (pounded)
3 cm each rampa, lemon grass
1 sprig curry leaves
1 tsp garam masala
1 cup water

¼ tsp turmeric powder
4 green chillies (slit)
2 cm piece ginger (crushed)
oil for frying
1 tbsp curry powder
marble sized tamarind
salt to taste

Method
1. Cut the brinjals into thin slices 10 cm long. Soak in water for two minutes. Drain and squeeze out the water from the brinjals. Season with turmeric powder and salt.
2. Fry the brinjals to a golden brown colour and set aside.
3. Dissolve the tamarind inthe cup of water and strain.
4. Fry the onions, garlic, chillies, ginger, curry leaves, rampa and lemon grass in a frying pan with 4 table spoons of oil. When the onions are lightly browned add the maldive fish and fry for one more minute.
5. Add tamarind juice, curry powder, and salt. Bring to boil and simmer for two minutes. Mix in the fried brinjals and garam masala. Cover and simmer for a further 5 minutes, until the curry becomes dry.

Bottle Gourd Curry

Cook as in ash pumpkin curry.

Bread fruit Curry

1 bread fruit (medium)
2 green chillies (chopped)
3 cups thin coconut milk
Tempering
1 tbsp onions (sliced)
½ tsp mustard seeds

4 red onions (sliced)
2 tsp curry powder
salt to taste

1 sprig curry leaves
1 tbsp oil

Method
1. Skin and cut the bread fruit into 2 cm cubes. Rinse the cut pieces.
2. Place bread fruit, onions, chillies, curry powder, coconut milk and salt in a pan , bring to boil. Stir, cover and cook on low heat until the bread fruit is soft. Simmer on low heat.
3. Temper the onions, mustard and curry leaves in oil until the onions are browned. Pour over the bread fruit, stir and remove from the heat.

Brinjal Curry

250g brinjal
2 green chillies (slit)
2 cup thick coconut milk

4 red onions (sliced)
2 tsp curry powder
salt to taste

Method

1. Cut the brinjal into strips 5 cm long and soak in water for 2 minutes.
2. Drain and squeeze out the water from the brinjals. Cover and cook the brinjals, onions, chillies, curry powder, salt and coconut milk in a pan over medium heat for 10 minutes stirring occasionally. Turn off the heat as soon as the gravy thickens and the oil separates in the curry.

Brinjal Kulambu

250g brinjal
1 large onion (sliced)
4 cloves garlic (halved)
¼ tsp black gram dhal
½ tsp sweet cumin
1 tbsp curry powder
1 cup thick coconut milk
salt to taste

½ tsp turmeric powder
3 dry chillies (broken up)
1 sprig curry leaves
1½ tsp fenugreek
¼ tsp mustard seeds
2 cup thin coconut milk
marble sized tamarind
oil for frying

Method

1. Cut the brinjals into strips 5 cm long and soak in water for two minutes. Drain and squeeze out the water from the brinjals.

   Season with turmeric powder and salt.

2. Deep fry to a golden brown colour and keep aside.

3. Dissolve the tamarind in the thin coconut milk and strain.

4. Sauté onions, dry chillies, garlic and curry leaves in one table spoon oil. As the onions start to brown add the fenugreek, black gram dhal, cumin, mustard seeds and stir fry for a minute.

5. Add the tamarind juice, curry powder, thick coconut milk and salt to the spice mixture. Bring to boil, reduce heat and cook for 15 minutes.

6. Mix in the fried brinjal and simmer for 5 minutes or until the gravy has thickened to your liking.

Variation

Ladies fingers, potatoes, drumsticks, or a mixture of these vegetables could also be used instead of the brinjals. Tomatoes could also be used, however they need not be deep fried.

Fried Brinjal

250g brinjal
4 tbsp sesame oil
salt to taste

1 tsp curry powder
1 tbsp onions (sliced)

Method

1. Cut the brinjal into 2 cm cubes and soak in water for two minutes. Drain and squeeze out the water from the brinjals. Season with curry powder and salt.
2. Heat the oil in a frying pan and shallow fry until the brinjals are golden brown and quite dry.
3. Add onions and continue frying until the onions are crisp.

Variation

Crispy Fried Brinjal: If you prefer the brinjals to be crisp, deep fry them in coconut oil or vegetable oil and drain off excess oil.

Brinjal Curry (White)

Cook as brinjal curry. But, instead of curry powder use more green chillies and quarter tsp of turmeric powder. Maldive fish broken into small pieces, dried prawns or quarted crabs may be added if preferred.

Dhal Curry

250g dhal
2 tbs sliced onions
2 tsp curry powder
1 sprig curry leaves
¼ tsp mustard seeds
½ cup thick coconut milk
    (optional)

5 cups water
2 green chillies (slit)
4 cloves garlic (halved)
2 dry chillies
2 tbsp ghee or butter
salt to taste

Method

1. Wash and destone the dhal. Place the dhal, 1 table spoon of onion, green chillies and water in a pan, bring to boil and simmer until the dhal is soft.

2. Add curry powder, garlic, salt and coconut milk if desired. Mix well and continue cooking on low heat.

3. Fry the onions, dry chillies and curry leaves in ghee. When the onions are starting to brown add the mustard seeds, stir fry for half a minute, remove and stir into the dhal. Remove the dhal from the fire.

Variation

Cook the dhal till soft with onions, chillies and water.
Dissolve a marble sized tamarind in one cup of water and strain. Fry 1 tsp of white cumin, 1 tsp chilli powder and a few curry leaves in 2 tbsp oil for half a minute. Add the tamarind juice to the spice mixture and boil for 1 minute.
Add the dhal to this mixture, add the salt and simmer for 2 minutes. Remove from heat.

Dhal Curry II

250g toor dhal or black gram dhal
4 green chillies (chopped)
1 tsp garam masala
1 tsp fenugreek
½ tsp mustard seed
2 cups coconut milk
salt to taste

6 red onions (sliced)
1 sprig curry leaves
2 dry chillies (broken)
½ tsp sweet cumin
marble sized tamarind
2 tsp curry powder
oil for frying

Preparation

1. Wash and destone the dhal. Soak in water for 2 hours.

Method

1. Drain and grind the dhal into a coarse paste.
2. Add half the onions, half the curry leaves (finely chopped), green chillies, garam masala and salt to the paste. Mix well. Shape the paste into 1 cm thick discs on stringhopper mats and steam for 10 minutes or till they are done.
3. Cut the steamed dhal paste into small cubes.
4. Dissolve the tamarind in the coconut milk and strain.
5. Fry the remaining onions, dry chillies and the rest of the curry leaves in oil. As the onions become soft add the fenugreek, cumin and mustard.
6. Stir in the dhal pieces as the mustard seeds start to crackle and cook for 5 minutes. Pour in the coconut milk (with tamarind) to the mixture together with the curry powder and salt. Bring to boil and simmer until the gravy thickens.

Dhal Curry III

250g toor dhal
50g butter
1½ tbsp gram flour
few chopped coriander leaves

5 cups boiling water
½ tsp white cumin
2 green chillies
salt to taste

Method

1. Clean and destone the dhal. Cook in water till the dhal becomes soft. Strain and retain excess water. Mash the dhal well and add the previously retained water. Mix well and set aside.
2. Temper the cumin in hot butter for few seconds and add to the dhal.
3. Mix the gram flour into a paste using 2-3 table spoons of water. Mix the paste with the dhal and simmer the curry for 5 minutes stirring occasionally.
4. Turn off the heat. Add the green chillies and the coriander leaves to the dhal and mix well.

Drumstick Curry

250g drumsticks
2 cup thick coconut milk
1 tbsp curry powder
salt to taste

2 tbsp onions (sliced)
1 cup thin coconut milk
250g shelled prawns
(optional)

Method

1. Cut the drumstick into 7 cm long pieces, skinning and removing the fibres at the same time. Split the drumsticks into two.
2. Wash and place in a pan with all other ingredients. Bring to boil, reduce heat and cook uncovered for 5 minutes.
3. Stir, cover and cook until the gravy is thick and the drumsticks are cooked.

Drumstick Varai

250g drumstick
2 broken up dry chillies
¼ tsp mustard seeds
2 tbsp scraped coconut
2 tbsp oil

1 tbsp sliced red onions
¼ tsp turmeric powder
1 sprig curry leaves
4 tbsp water
salt to taste

Method

1. Scrape out the soft part (kernel) of the drumstick and chop it.
2. Cook this with water on low heat till soft and the water is absorbed. Remove from the fire.
3. Add coconut, turmeric powder, and salt. Mix well.
4. Sauté in oil the mustard seeds, dry chillies, onions and curry leaves for two minutes in a frying pan.
5. Stir the drumstick mixture into the sautéed condiments. Cook on a low heat stirring occasionally until the mixture is quite dry.

Fried Jak Seeds

250g jak seeds
1 sprig curry leaves
salt to taste

1 tsp curry powder
1 tbsp sliced onions
oil for frying

Method

1. Choose matured jak seeds and halve them longitudinally. Peel and scrape off the red skin.
2. Wash the seeds and season with curry powder and salt.

3. Deep fry the jak seeds in hot oil for about two minutes until they are crisp and golden colour. Add the curry leaves and onions and fry for a minute. Remove from the oil, drain off oil and then place on absorbent paper.

Hint : If jak seeds are fried for too long they become hard and difficult to bite.

Sodhi

1 cup thin coconut milk
1 cup water
3 green chillies (sliced)
few curry leaves
¼ tsp turmeric powder
10 cm pieces of rampa, lemon grass & cinnamon

2 cups thick coconut milk
4 red onions (sliced)
1 tsp fenugreek
1 lime
salt to taste

Note: This is a basic recipe for sodhi to be served with stringhopper, pittu, rice etc. The gravy can be flavoured by adding different vegetables. Details are given under variations.

Method
1. Place all the ingredients other than the coconut milk and lime in a pan. Bring to boil and simmer for 3 minutes.
2. Add all the coconut milk, simmer for 3 minutes, remove from the fire and add the lime juice.

Variations
Potato Sodhi: Add boiled and diced potatoes with the coconut milk.
Tomato Sodhi : Add sliced tomatoes to the basic recipe. Add ½ a lime juice at the end.
Egg Sodhi : Add hard boiled eggs cut into half with the coconut milk.

Green Gram Dhal Curry

250g green gram dhal
1 tbs. sliced onions
2 tsp curry powder
1 cup thick coconut milk
Tempering:
½ tsp mustard seeds
sprig of curry leaves

5 cups water
2 chopped green chillies
4 cloves garlic
salt to taste

1 dry chilli (broken up)
2 tbsp butter

Method

1. Clean and destone the dhal as necessary. Dry roast the dhal. (see page 31 for roasted green gram dhal).
2. Cook the dhal in water until it becomes soft. Add the onions, green chillies, curry powder, garlic, coconut milk and salt. Mix well and simmer for 5 minutes.
3. Fry the mustard, onions, dry chilli and curry leaves in hot butter until the onions are golden brown in colour. Stir this into the dhal and turn off the heat to the dhal.

Variation

Make a coarsely ground paste using ½ tsp of pepper, 1 tsp of white cumin and 3 pips of garlic. Add this instead of the fried condiments. Simmer for 2 minutes before taking off the fire.

Leeks Varai

Prepare as spring onion varai using 250g leeks.

Kadalai Curry

100g potato
5 cm piece ginger (minced)
¼ tsp turmeric powder
1 large onion (chopped)
1 tsp curry powder
200g chopped tomatoes

250g kadalai (chick pea)
½ cup water
2 tbsp oil
few curry leaves
1 tsp garam masala
salt to taste

Preparation

1. Wash, destone and soak the kadalai preferably overnight or for 10 hours.

Method

1. Wash again and then cover with water and cook till soft. Drain the water.
2. Peel the potatoes and dice them into 1 cm cubes. Place the diced potato in boiling salted water, cook until soft and drain.
3. Grind ½ cup of kadalai, ½ cup of water, ginger and turmeric to a smooth paste in a blender.
4. Using a heavy pan sauté the onions and curry leaves in oil until the onions are translucent. Mix in the curry powder and stir fry for a minute before adding the remaining boiled kadalai, the paste, potatoes and tomatoes. Stir and cook until the mixture is thick and creamy.
5. Season with garam masala and salt before removing from the fire.

Karanai Yam Curry

250g karanai yam
2 green chillies (chopped)
½ tsp fenugreek
¼ tsp mustard
3 cups coconut milk
salt to taste

2 tbsp sliced onions
1 sprig of curry leaves
¼ tsp sweet cumin
marble sized tamarind
2 tsp curry powder
oil for frying

Method

1. Peel and cut the yam into small pieces. Wash well and drain.
2. Dissolve the tamarind in one cup of water and strain.
3. Deep fry the yam pieces in hot oil until they are crisp and golden in colour. Drain and place on the absorbent paper to remove any excess oil.
4. Heat 2 tbsp oil in a pan and fry the onions, chillies and curry leaves until the onions are browned then add the fenugreek, cumin and mustard seeds and fry for one more minute.
5. Pour in the coconut milk and the tamarind water together with the curry powder and salt. Bring to boil and cook on reduced heat for 5 minutes.
6. Mix in the fried yam pieces cover and cook on low heat until the gravy thickens.

Variation

Lime juice could be added instead of tamarind however the lime juice should only be added after taking the curry off the fire on completion of cooking.

Lady's Finger Curry

250g lady's finger
3 green chillies (chopped)
¼ tsp turmeric powder (optional)
salt to taste

1 tbsp sliced onions
1 cup coconut milk
1 tbsp lime juice
(optional)

Method

1. Wash and cut the vegetable into 3 cm pieces.
2. Place all the ingredients in a pan and cook on a medium heat for 10 minutes stirring occasionally.

Hint:
To avoid the jelly like consistency of the curry add lime juice and cook.

Boiled Lady's Fingers

250g lady's finger
¼ tsp pepper powder

1 cup water
salt to taste

Method

1. Choose tender lady's fingers. Wash and cut into 7 cm pieces.
2. Place in a pan with water and salt and cook over a medium heat until all the water is absorbed. Sprinkle the pepper powder, stir and remove from the fire.

Lady's Finger Kulambu

Cook as brinjal kulambu using lady's fingers (vendikai) cut into 3 cm pieces.

Fried Lady's Fingers

Fry as for plantain chips. See ash plantain fried variation I.

Long Beans Curry

250g long beans
2 chopped green chillies
2 cup coconut milk
salt to taste

2 tbsp sliced onions
2 tsp curry powder
few curry leaves

Method

1. Choose young beans. If the beans are matured use only their seeds.
2. Break off the heads and tails of the beans drawing out the fibre running down the sides of the beans. Break into 3 cm pieces and wash them.
3. Place in a pan with all other ingredients bring to boil, stir, lower the heat and cook for 5 minutes uncovered. Cover and continue cooking until the gravy has thickened and the beans are cooked.

Murunga Leaves Varai

Cook as spring onion varai using 3 cups of finely chopped murunga leaves.

Potato Curry

250g potatoes
2 green chillies (chopped)
1 sprig of curry leaves
4 cardamoms
1 tsp fragrant powder
salt to taste

4 red onions (sliced)
2 tsp curry powder
¼ tsp fenugreek
2 cups coconut milk
1 lime

Method

1. Wash the potatoes and place in a pan with water and boil until the potatoes are soft. Peel and cut into 3 cm cubes.
2. Put all the ingredients excluding the potatoes, fragrant powder and the lime in a pan, bring to boil, stir and cook over medium heat for five minutes. Add in the potatoes, cover and simmer for 5 minutes.
3. Mix the fragrant powder, stir, cover and cook for a minute before removing from the fire.
4. Once the curry has cooled squeeze the lime juice into the curry.

Potato Kulambu

Cook as brinjal kulambu using potatoes.

Fried Potatoes

250g potatoes
1 tbsp onions (sliced)
4 tbsp sesame oil
1 tsp curry powder
salt to taste

Method

1. Peel and cut the potatoes into 2 cm cubes. Wash, drain and season with curry powder and salt.
2. Heat the oil in a frying pan and fry the potato pieces in hot oil for 2 minutes without stirring.
3. Stir and continue frying stirring occasionally, until the potatoes are cooked.
4. Add the onion and cook until they are browned. Remove from the fire and drain off excess oil.

Plantain Flower Curry

1 plantain flower
1 tbsp onion (sliced)
1 sprig curry leaves
1 tsp curry powder
2 tbsp oil
2 tsp salt
1 dry chilli (broken up)
marble sized tamarind
1 cup coconut milk

Preparation

1. Discard the mature petals and finely chop the plantain flower. Season with salt and leave for 10 minutes.
2. Squeeze the seasoned vegetable to remove as much fluid as possible and set aside.

Method
1. Dissolve the tamarind in the coconut milk and strain.
2. Heat the oil and temper the onions, chilli and curry leaves. Add the chopped flower and stir fry for a minute.
3. Mix in the coconut milk (with tamarind) and curry powder. Stir well. Cover and cook for 10 minutes on a slow fire or until cooked.
4. Salt to taste before removing from the fire.

Plantain Flower Varai

1 plantain flower
½ cup scraped coconut
½ tsp curry powder (optional)
2 tbsp oil

2 tsp salt
2 broken up dry chillies
2 tbsp sliced onions
few curry leaves

Preparation

1. Choose a fresh flower and discard all the mature petals. Finely chop the flower, season with salt and leave for 10 minutes.

Method

1. Squeeze the seasoned vegetable to remove as much of fluid as possible. Mix in the scraped coconut and the optional curry powder.
2. Heat the oil in a frying pan and fry the onions, chillies and curry leaves. As the onions start to brown, add the flower mixture and stir.
3. Reduce to low heat and cook stirring occasionally until the mixture is quite dry.
4. Check and add salt if required before removing from the fire.

Sambar

100g dhal
1 tsp curry powder
marble sized tamarind
1 cup thick coconut milk
2 green chillies (slit)
few curry leaves
½ tsp mustard seeds
1 tbsp oil

500g mixed vegetables
4 tsp sambar powder
5 cups water
6 red onions (sliced)
2 dry chillies (broken up)
½ tsp sweet cumin
1 pinch of asafoetida
salt to taste

Preparation

1. Wash, peel and dice the carrots, potatoes, pumpkin, ash plantain, and turnips.
2. Break the heads and tails of the beans and remove the fibre on the sides. Slice the beans.
3. Slice the tomatoes. Cut the brinjal into 5 cm long thin slices. Shred the cabbage.
4. Cut the murunga into 7 cm pieces and split into two.
5. Cut the lady's fingers into 3 cm pieces. Break the cauliflower into bite size pieces.
6. Dissolve the tamarind in a little water and strain.
7. Deep fry the prepared brinjals, murunga and the ladys fingers in hot oil to a golden brown colour.

Method

1. Wash the dhal and place in a pan along with all the vegetables (except tomatoes and fried vegetables), salt, curry powder, green chillies, water and half the onions. Cook over medium heat until the vegetables are cooked and the dhal is soft.

2. Add the tomatoes, fried vegetables, coconut milk, tamarind water and the sambar powder. Cook for 5 more minutes.
3. Fry the onions, chillies, cumin, mustard, asafoetida and the curry leaves in hot oil. Pour the fried condiments over the sambar, mix well and cook for one more minute.

Snake Gourd Varai

250g snake gourd
2 broken up dry chillies
½ tsp mustard seeds
¼ cup scraped coconut
salt to taste

1 tbsp sliced onions
1 sprig of curry leaves
¼ tsp turmeric powder
2 tbsp oil

Method

1. Scrape the skin off the gourd and split into two and discard the seeds. Wash and chop it finely and then steam for 5 minutes.
2. Mix the steamed gourd with salt, turmeric and coconut. Fry the mustard seeds, onions, chillies and curry leaves in hot oil. As the onions brown add the gourd mixture and fry stirring occasionally until the mixture is quite dry.

Snake Gourd Curry

250g snake gourd
1 tbsp sliced onions
¼ tsp turmeric powder
2 cups coconut milk

100g dhal
2 chopped green chillies
5 cm piece cinnamon
salt to taste

Method

1. Wash the dhal.
2. Scrape the skin off the snake gourd, split into two and discard the seeds. Cut into small pieces and wash.
3. Place the dhal, gourd pieces, and all other ingredients in a pan, cover and cook over a medium heat, stirring occasionally. Turn off heat as soon as the gourd is soft.

Snake Gourd Curry II

250g snake gourd
2 chopped green chillies
1 cup thick coconut milk
salt to taste

1 tbsp sliced onions
1 tsp curry powder
1 sprig of curry leaves

Method

1. Scrape the skin off the gourd, split into two and discard the seeds. Cut into small pieces and wash.
2. Place all the ingredients in a pan, bring to boil, stir, cover and cook over medium heat until the gravy thickens.

Ridge Gourd Curry

250g ridge gourd
2 cloves garlic (crushed)
3 cm piece ginger (chopped)
2 green chillies (chopped)
¼ tsp mustard seeds
1 tbsp maldive fish powdered
¼ tsp turmeric powder or
½ lime

1 tbs. sliced onions
¼ tsp fenugreek
¼ tsp sweet cumin
1 sprig curry leaves
½ cup coconut milk
2 tbsp oil
¼ tsp curry powder
salt to taste

Method

1. Choose tender ridge gourds. Peel and cut them into 3 cm cubes before washing them.
2. Heat the oil and temper the garlic, ginger, onions, chillies and curry leaves. As the onions start to brown add the fenugreek, cumin and mustard, temper for 1 more minute.
3. Stir in the ridge gourd. Follow this with turmeric powder and salt ensuring that they are well mixed in.
4. Cover and cook on low fire for 1 minute. Mix the coconut milk and maldive fish. Simmer until the gravy thickens.
4. Remove the curry from the fire and add lime juice.

Spring Onion Varai

250g spring onion
1 tbsp sliced onions
1 tsp white cumin
salt to taste

¼ cup scraped coconut
2 broken up dry chillies
2 tbsp oil

Method

1. Clean, wash and dry the spring onion. Cut it finely and mix with the coconut and salt.
2. Fry the onions and chillies in hot oil. When the onions are slightly browned add the cumin and stir fry for half a minute. Add the onion mixture and continue frying for 5 minutes stirring occasionally.

Spinach Curry

1 bundle spinach
2 green chillies
½ cup thick coconut milk
1 lime

5 onions
3 cloves garlic (optional)
¼ cup water
salt to taste

Method

1. Clean and wash the tender spinach.
2. Cook the spinach, onions, chillies, and garlic (if desired) in water until the water is absorbed. Stir twice during the cooking.
3. Remove from the cooker and mash the spinach mixture with the back of a spoon.

4. Add coconut milk and salt. Simmer for 2 minutes. Remove from the fire and mix in the lime juice.

Sweet Pumpkin Curry

250g sweet pumpkin
2 green chillies (chopped)
1 sprig of curry leaves
½ cup thick coconut milk
salt to taste

4 onions (sliced)
2 cloves garlic (chopped)
1 tsp curry powder
(optional)

Method

1. Peel and cut the pumpkin into 3 cm pieces.
2. Wash and put all the ingredients into a pan, bring to the boil, stir and reduce the heat. Cover and cook on a slow fire until the pumpkin is soft.
3. If preferred squeeze the lime juice into the curry after removing from the fire.

Tapioca Curry

250g tapioca
4 green chillies (chopped)
2 cups coconut milk
1 tsp curry powder   or
salt to taste

4 red onions (sliced)
1 sprig curry leaves
½ lime
¼ tsp turmeric powder

Method

1. Peel and cut the tapioca into 3 cm cubes. Wash and cook in an uncovered pan of water until the yam is soft. Drain off excess water.
2. Using a pan cook the onions, chillies, curry leaves, curry powder or turmeric powder, coconut milk and salt for 5 minutes on medium heat.
3. Add the tapioca pieces, stir cover and simmer until the gravy thickens.
4. Remove from the fire and add the lime juice.

Caution: Never eat tapioca with ginger, as the combination is poisonous.

Tapioca Chips

Prepare as for Ash Plantain Chips.

Tomato Curry

250g tomatoes
2 green chillies (chopped)

4 onions (sliced)
4 cloves garlic (sliced)

2 cups coconut milk
2 tsp curry powder
salt to taste

½ tsp fenugreek
1 sprig curry leaves

Method

1. Wash and cut the tomatoes into large pieces.
2. Place all the ingredients in a pan, bring to boil, reduce heat, stir, cover and cook till the gravy is thick.

Tomato Kulambu

250g tomatoes
2 green chillies (chopped)
3 cm ginger (crushed)
1 tsp fenugreek
½ tsp mustard seeds
3 cups coconut milk
1 tsp fragrant powder
salt to taste

4 onions (sliced)
4 cloves garlic crushed)
1 sprig curry leaves
½ tsp sweet cumin
¼ tsp black gram dhal
1 tbsp curry powder
2 tbsp oil

Method

1. Wash and cut the tomatoes into large pieces.
2. Heat the oil in a pan and fry the onions, chillies, garlic, ginger and curry leaves. As the onions begin to brown add the fenugreek, black gram dhal, cumin and the mustard. Stir fry for a minute.
3. Mix in the tomatoes, salt and curry powder, stir well and cook for two minutes. Pour in the coconut milk with the fragrant

Venthayak Kulambu

Prepare as tomato kulambu omit the tomatoes and increase the onions to 10 and the fenugreek to 1 table spoon.

SAMBALS
PACHCHADIS
&
CHUTNEYS

Ash Plantain Sambal

250g plantains
½ lime or 1 cup curd or both
1 tbsp powdered maldive fish
      (optional)
1 sprig curry leaves

2 large onions (sliced)
½ cup thick coconut milk
4 green chillies (chopped)
¼ turmeric powder
salt to taste

Method

1. Wash the plantains. Boil or deep fry the whole plantains until they are soft. Remove, peel the skin and mash the plantains while they are hot.

2. Lightly mash the onions, chillies, chopped curry leaves, maldive fish, turmeric powder, lime juice and salt in a bowl.

3. Thoroughly mix the pulp, coconut milk and curd with the mashed condiments.

Hint: The mixing can also be done in a blender or a food processor. Put all the ingredients into the blender or processor and mince for a short time.

Brinjal Sambal

250g brinjal
4 green chillies (chopped)
3 cm ginger (crushed)
½ lime or 1 cup curd or both
1 tbsp maldive fish (optional)

2 large onions (chopped)
2 cloves garlic (crushed)
1 sprig curry leaves
½ cup thick coconut milk
salt to taste

Method

1. Smear a little oil on the skin of the brinjals and roast on a gas flame or over a charcoal fire till soft.
2. Skin the roasted brinjals and mash the pulp.
3. Break the maldive fish into small pieces.
4. Lightly mash the onions, chillies, garlic, ginger, curry leaves, maldive fish, lime juice and salt in a bowl.
5. Mix in the brinjal pulp, curd and the coconut milk into the mashed condiments.

Brinjal Sambal II

250g brinjal
2 large onions, finely sliced
2 medium tomatoes
1 tbsp maldive fish
¼ cup thick coconut milk
salt to taste

¼ tsp turmeric powder
4 green chillies
    (finelychopped)
1 tbsp lime juice
oil for frying

Method

1. Cut the brinjals into small pieces and soak in the water. Drain and squeeze the brinjals to remove water. Season with salt and turmeric powder.
2. Fry brinjals in hot oil to a golden colour. Remove and drain off oil.
3. Break the maldive fish into small pieces and chop the tomatoes.
4. Mix the onions, chillies, maldive fish, tomatoes, lime juice, salt and coconut milk in a bowl. Add in the brinjal and mix well.

Bitter Gourd Sambal

Prepare as brinjal sambal II. Remove the seeds before frying the gourd.

Carrot Sambal

250g carrots
6 red onions (finely sliced)
1 tbsp powdered maldive fish
3 cm ginger (finely chopped)

3 green chillies (chopped)
3 tbsp scraped coconut
juice of a lime
salt to taste

1. Peel, wash and grate the carrots. Mix all the ingredients together. Alternatively put all the ingredients in a food processor and mince for 2 minutes.

Coconut Sambal

2 cups scraped coconut
1 tbsp pounded maldive fish (optional)
½ lime

10 dry chillies
5 red onions

salt to taste

Method

1. Grind chillies and salt to a powder. Add the coconut, maldive fish, onion and continue grinding until the ingredients are completely blended together. Remove and add the lime juice.

Variation:

Place all the ingredients in a blender and blend until the chillies are completely powdered.

Prepare as above with the dry chillies and curry leaves fried separately in hot oil to a crisp. Use tamarind pulp instead of the lime juice.

Coriander Sambal

3 tbsp coriander
4 red onions
salt to taste

2 dry chillies
10 cm piece coconut

Method

1. Dry roast (lightly) the coriander, chillies and coconut pieces.
2. Grind the coriander, chillies and salt to a smooth paste with little water in a grind stone or a blender.
3. Add the coconut pieces and grind, then add the onions and continue to grind the mixture to a smooth paste.
4. Remove this mixture and hand mix to ensure even distribution of the ingredients.

Coriander Sambal II

2 cups coriander leaves (chopped)
2 tbsp black gram dhal
2 tbsp oil
small marble sized tamarind

6 dry chillies
pinch of a asafoetida
½ tsp mustard seeds
salt to taste

Method

1. Fry the chillies, black gram dhal and asafoetida until the chillies become brown in oil.
2. Pound, grind or blend (using a blender) all the ingredients except the mustard to a coarse paste.
3. Fry the mustard seeds in oil until they crackle and mix into the sambal.

Cucumber Sambal

1 large cucumber
½ tsp salt
2 tbsp mint leaves (chopped)
1 tbsp olive oil

1 tsp sugar
1½ cup curd
1 tsp pepper powder

Preparation

1. Peel the cucumber, split into two and remove all the seeds.
2. Cut into small strips, mix with sugar and salt and leave to drain in a colander for 30 minutes.

Method

1. Mix the prepared cucumber with curd, mint and freshly made pepper.
2. Place in a serving dish and sprinkle the oil evenly over the sambal.

Curd Pachchadi

1 cup thick curd
3 green chillies
½ tsp mustard seeds
1 sprig curry leaves
salt to taste

3 cm piece ginger
2 tbsp scraped coconut
pinch of asafoetida
1 tbsp oil

Method

1. Grind the chillies, ginger, and coconut to a fine paste.
2. Beat the curd. Add the ground paste to the curd and mix well.
3. Fry the mustard, asafoetida and curry leaves in hot oil and mix into the curd mixture.

Ginger Pachchadi

10 dry chillies
3 cm piece ginger
½ lime

2 cups scraped coconut
5 red onions
salt to taste

Method

1. Roast the ginger over a gas flame or charcoal fire. Peel the skin and wash.
2. Pound, grind or blend (in a blender) the chillies and salt into a powder. Add the ginger and continue. Follow this with coconut and onions and continue until the mix becomes a smooth paste.
3. Place in a dish, squeeze the lime juice and mix it in.

Green Chilli Pachchadi

15 green chillies
3 cm piece ginger (chopped)
½ tsp mustard seeds
1 lime
salt to taste

2 cups scraped coconut
5 red onions
1 sprig curry leaves
1 tbsp oil

Method

1. Using a blender blend the green chillies, ginger, onions, coconut, salt and ½ cup of water into a smooth paste.
2. Fry the mustard and curry leaves in hot oil until the mustard starts to pop. Pour this over the chilli mixture.
3. Add the lime juice and mix.

Katta Sambal

10 dry chillies
1 tbsp maldive fish (powdered)
salt to taste

5 red onions
½ lime

Method

1. Grind the chillies and salt to a fine powder. Add the onions and grind into a coarse paste.
2. Mix in the maldive fish and grind lightly.
3. Remove from the blender and add the lime juice to the sambal.

Mint Sambal

2 cups mint leaves
6 red onions
6 cm piece ginger
½ lime
salt to taste

2 tbsp scraped coconut
4 green chillies
2 clove garlic
3 tbsp water

Method

1. Using a blender grind all the ingredients to a smooth paste and add lime juice.

Seeni Sambal

250g onions (finely sliced)
4 cloves garlic (finely sliced)
1 cm ginger (finely chopped)
50g maldive fish (pounded)
3 cm rampa & lemon grass
1 tsp sugar
1 cup coconut milk (optional)

10 dry chillies
20 cardamoms
big marble sized tamarind
1 sprig curry leaves
3 cm piece cinnamon
5 tbsp oil
salt to taste

Method

1. Grind the cardamom with the chillies. Mix the salt with the onions.
2. Dissolve the tamarind in one cup of water or in coconut milk and strain.
3. Fry one table spoon of onions, garlic, ginger, rampa, lemon grass, curry leaves and the cinnamon piece in 2 table spoons of oil until the onions are browned.
4. Pour in the remainder of the oil and when this is hot add in the maldive fish and the rest of the onions. Stir well and fry till the onions are transparent.
5. Add the chilli powder and stir fry for 2 minutes. Mix in the tamarind juice and simmer for 5 minutes.
6. Add the sugar and stir well for a minute and remove from the fire.

Sweet Pumpkin Sambal

250g sweet pumpkin
2 big onions (finely sliced)
2 tbsp thick coconut milk
4 green chillies (finely chopped)

¼ cup water
1 sprig curry leaves
1 lime
salt to taste

Method

1. Peel the pumpkin and remove all the seeds. Cut into small cubes and wash.
2. Boil with water over a low fire until the pumpkin is soft and all the water has been absorbed.
3. Mash the pumpkin and mix thoroughly with all other ingredients.

Thuthuwalai Sambal
(Kattu Wal Battu Sambol)

2 cups thuthuwalai leaves
4 red onions
½ lime

4 green chillies
2 tbsp scraped coconut
salt to taste

Method

1. Wash the leaves and dry roast in a pan on a slow fire with the onions, chillies and coconut until the thorns are soft.
2. Grind the mixture into a smooth paste and mix in the lime juice.

Tomato Sambal

250g tomatoes
2 green chillies finely chopped
1 sprig curry leaves
salt to taste

2 big onions finely sliced
½ lime juice
1 tbsp thick coconut milk
or curd

Method

1. Chop the tomatoes into small pieces.
2. Mix with all other ingredients.

Tomato Chutney

250g tomatoes
2 big onions (chopped)
few coriander leaves

10 dry chillies
3 cloves garlic
salt to taste

Method

1. Roast the tomatoes over a iron griddle or charcoal fire and peel the skin.
2. Dry roast the chillies in a frying pan.
3. Place all the ingredients in a blender and blend together to a coarse paste.

Vallarai (Gotukola) Sambal

Method

1. Prepare as thuthuwalai sambal using valaarai leaves instead of thuthuwalai leaves.
2. Alternatively wash and finely chop the leaves, onions and chillies.
3. Mix the chopped ingredients with the coconut, salt and lime juice.

   Vallarai : Sinhala : Gotukola

PICKLES AND VADAHAMS

Lime Pickle

250g limes
1 tbsp fenugreek
3 dry chillies
¼ bottle lime juice

salt
1 tbsp sweet cumin
2 cm piece turmeric
10g green chillies

Preparation

1. Split the limes into 4 without completely separating the pieces. Keep the pieces joined together at the base.
2. Fill the split limes with powdered salt, put them in a bottle with green chillies (slightly slit) and leave for 3 days.
3. After 3 days dry the limes in sunlight till they are very dry.

Method

1. Dry roast the fenugreek, cumin, chillies and turmeric over slow fire until they are golden in colour and powder them.
2. Put the dried limes back in the bottle and pour the lime juice mixed with the condiment powder.

Plantain Flower Vadaham

Use finely chopped Plantain Flower instead of margosa flower and make as above.

Curd Chillies

500g green chillies 2 cup curd
3 tbsp salt (powdered)

Method

1. Make a small slit in the chillies.
2. Beat the curd with the salt in an earthen vessel Add the slit chillies to the curd, mix well, cover and keep for 3 days.
3. Take the chillies after 3 days leaving the excess curd in the pot and sun dry them for a few days, until they are very dry. At the end of each day's drying, put the chillies back in the curd pot and cover. Repeat this until all the curd has been absorbed by the chillies. Once all the curd has been absorbed there is no need to return the chillies to the pot at the end of the day's drying.
4. Store in an airtight container and deep fry in hot oil when needed.

Vadaham

1 cup dried margosa flower
6 dry chillies
1 sprig curry leaves

¼ cup black gram dhal
1 tsp sweet cumin
salt to taste

Method

1. Soak the dhal for 4 hours and wash. Grind it into a coarse paste.
2. Grind the chillies into a coarse powder, crush the cumin and then put all the ingredients in a bowl and mix well.
3. Taking one table spoon of the mixture at a time shape it into a ball and then flatten it into a disc about 8 mm thick.
4. Sun dry the discs until quite dry.
5. Store in an air tight container. Deep fry in hot oil when needed.

DESSERTS

Carrot Halwa

500g carrot
100g ghee
pinch cardamom powder
2 tbsp cadju (chopped)

300g sugar
5 cups milk
2 tbsp raisin

Method

1. Peel and grate the carrot finely.
2. Cook the carrot, milk and sugar in a pan over a medium heat stirring occasionally until the liquid has evaporated.
3. Add the ghee, raisin, cadju and cardamom powder, fry for 15-20 minutes stirring constantly until the mixture is dry and reddish in colour.
4. Serve hot or cold.

Curd and Treacle

1 pot of fresh curd   treacle or honey

Method
1. Spoon the curd into the serving bowls, pour the treacle or honey over it and serve.

Custard

3 cups milk
3 tbsp sugar

3 eggs
1 tsp vanilla

Method
1. Beat the eggs and the sugar together.
2. Warm the milk, add it to the egg mixture with the vanilla and beat.
3. Cook this mixture stirring continuously in a bath of boiling water until it thickens.

Fruit Salad

1 mango
1 apple
3 plantains
100g grapes
1 lemon
2 tsp vanilla

½ papaw
½ pineapple
1 orange
100g sugar
½ cup water

Method
1. Wash, peel and dice the mangoes, papaw, apple and pine apple into small pieces.
2. Peel the plantains and slice them. Cut the lemon in half. Squeeze the juice from one half on the plaintain slices and thoroughly coat them. Save the lemon rind for use later.
3. Peel the oranges, remove white skin, remove the pips and cut the fruit into sections. Save the rind for use later.
4. If the grapes are small use them whole, if not cut them into two and remove the seeds.
5. Cut the lemon and orange rind into thin strips, mix it with the water and simmer for 5 minutes. Mix in the sugar, vanilla and the juice from the other half of the lemon. Stir until the sugar is dissolved and allow to cool. To add a touch of luxury to the salad mix in some sherry, brandy or wine.
6. Mix the prepared fruits in a bowl. Strain the sugar syrup over the fruits and chill well before serving.

Hint : The salad could be served with custard or cream.

Kesari

1 cup semolina
pinch of cardamom powder
1 tbsp cadju (chopped)
pinch of kesari powder

2 cups sugar
1 cup ghee
1 tbsp plums
2 cups boiling water

Method

1. Separately fry the cadju and plums in 2 table spoons of hot ghee.

2. Using a pan roast the semolina in 1 table spoon of ghee until it turns a golden colour. Add the water and the kesari powder, cook till the semolina is soft.

3. Mix in the sugar and cook for 5 minutes stirring continuously. Add the rest of the ghee and cook for 3 minutes.

4. Mix the cardamom powder, cadju and plums into the mixture. Spread in a greased tray to a thickness of 1.5 cm. Cut into squares and serve hot or cold.

Payasam

200g sago
1 ltr milk or coconut milk
4 tbsp ghee or butter
1 tbsp cadju nuts (chopped)
2 cups water

10g semiya
100g sugar
5 cardamom (powdered)
1 tbsp plums

Method

1. Roast the sago in 2 tbsp ghee to a golden colour.

2. Fry the cadju and plums separately in ghee.
3. Cook the sago in water until it is transparent. Add semiya and milk, cook until the mixture thickens slightly.
4. Mix in the sugar and the cardamom powder and cook for 5 minutes.
4. Mix the cadju and plums into the sago mixture and serve hot or cold.

Rasawalli Pudding (King Yam)

500g rasawalli yam
1 cup thick coconut milk
salt to taste

100g sugar
2 cups thin coconut milk

Method

1. Peel and cut the yam into thin slices. Wash well and cook in a pan with the thin coconut milk until soft.
2. Remove from the fire and mash the yam with the back of a spoon. Add thick coconut milk and sugar, cook until the sugar has dissolved and the milk has boiled.
3. Serve hot or cold. Once cold the mixture will become a smooth firm paste.

Semiya Payasam

Make as above using 300g semiya instead of the sago.

Woodapple Cream

2 large ripe woodapples
3 cups coconut milk or water

3 tbsp sugar
1/8 tsp salt

Method

1. Break open the fruits and scoop the pulp out.

2. Liquidize the pulp with all other ingredients, pour into the serving bowl and chill well before serving.

Yoghurt Whip

1 cup fruit puree (see method)
sugar to taste

1 cup yoghurt

Method: **Puree**

1. Using soft fruits: Peel and cut the fruits into pieces and blend in a blender or mash.

2. Using hard fruits: Boil them with sugar and blend in a blender or mash.

3. Using canned fruits: Strain off the syrup and blend in a blender or mash.

4. The puree could be made up of a combination of the above. Add sugar if required.

5. Chill the yoghurt well. Add the yoghurt to the puree and beat well. If liked fold in a stiffly beaten egg white into the yoghurt mix.

6. Spoon it into the serving bowls and serve immediately. Decorate with pieces of the fruit used in the puree.

SNACKS AND REFRESHMENTS

Achchu Murukku

2 cups roasted rice flour
2 cups coconut milk (approx)
1 cup sugar
oil for frying

¾ cup roasted black gram flour
½ cup water
salt to taste

Method

1. Sieve both flours together and mix in the salt.
2. Boil the coconut milk. Remove from fire.
3. Add the hot coconut milk little by little to the flour and mix using the handle of a wooden spoon till it becomes a firm dough. If required add more boiled coconut milk.
4. Fill the achchu murukku mould and squeeze the dough on to a greased tray. Cut into 10 cm long pieces and deep fry in hot oil until crisp.
5. Make a sugar syrup to a stringy consistency by boiling a solution of sugar and water. Test the thickness of the syrup by placing one drop in cold water and seeing if it solidifies.
6. Remove the syrup from the fire and pour over the cold murukku and mix well until all the murukku pieces are coated with the sugar syrup.

Hint : To get golden brown murukku use white rice flour.

Adai

1 cup rice
6 dry chillies
1 cup toor dhal,
4 green chillies(chopped)
4 onions (finely chopped)
salt to taste

1 cup black gram dhal,
1 cup green gram dhal
1 cup gram dhal
sprig of curry leaves
sesame oil

Preparation

1. Soak the rice and the dhals in water for 6 hours.

Method

1. Wash and grind all the dhal, rice, chillies and salt to a smooth paste adding water to make the batter have a pouring consistency. Add the onions and curry leaves.
2. Heat an iron griddle, smear with oil, pour a spoon full of batter and spread into a circle 10 cm in diameter.
3. Make a small cut in the middle and pour 2 tsp oil in and around the cut.
4. Turn and cook the other side. Serve with chutney.

Awal (Pressed Rice)

2 cups awal
2 tbsp jaggery

½ cup scraped coconut

Method

1. Wash and stone the awal if required. Soak in water for a few minutes or until soft.
2. Squeeze out excess water and mix with the other ingredients.

Bonda

250g potatoes
2 dry chillies
½ tsp mustard seeds
few curry leaves
1 cup gram flour
pinch of bicarbonate of soda
salt to taste

4 red onions (sliced)
1 green chilli
¼ tsp turmeric powder
¼ tsp turmeric powder
1 tbsp rice flour
oil for frying

Method

1. Wash and boil the potatoes. Peel and cut into small pieces or mash coarsely.

2. Heat 2 table spoons of oil in a pan, fry the mustard, turmeric and broken dry chillies for 10 seconds and add the onions and green chilli. Fry till the onions are golden brown in colour.

3. Mix in the potatoes, salt and curry leaves. Sprinkle a little water and cook until the mixture is well blended.

4. Remove from the fire and make lime sized balls out of the mixture.

5. Sieve and mix the rice flour and gram flour. Add the turmeric powder, salt, bicarbonate of soda and water. Mix into a thick smooth batter.

6. Dip the potato balls in the batter and deep fry in hot oil to a golden brown colour. Drain off all excess oil and serve hot.

Green Gram Balls

2 cups roasted green gram flour
2 cups scraped coconut(fine)
2 pinch cardamom powder or
½ tsp white cumin powder &
½ tsp pepper powder

½ cup parboiled rice
    (optional)
2 cups sugar
1½ cup water
oil for frying

For Batter
1 cup raw rice flour   or   steamed wheat flour
2 pinches turmeric powder   water for mixing
salt to taste

Method

1. Sun dry the scraped coconut till it is crisp and roast to a golden colour. Grind to a fine powder.

2. If using parboiled rice, dry roast the rice to a light brown colour and grind into a powder.

3. Sift the green gram flour and rice flour together. Add the ground coconut, spice powder and salt. Mix well.

4. Boil the sugar and water to make a light syrup and then combine this with the flour mixture. Mix well and make marble sized balls.

5. Mix the raw rice flour, turmeric powder, salt and sufficient water to make a medium batter.

6. Dip the flour balls in the batter and deep fry them in hot oil by dropping them in one by one. Fry till they are crisp.

Kolukattai

2 cups roasted rice flour
1 cups roasted green gram dhal
2 pinch cardamom powder
1 cup finely scraped coconut

200g jaggery
boiling water
salt to taste

Method

1. Wash and boil the dhal in 2 cups of water until it becomes soft and the water has been absorbed.
2. Cool it and thoroughly mix in the coconut, scraped jaggery, spice and salt. Set aside.
3. Sieve the flour and add salt. Mix the flour into a pliable dough using just enough boiling water. Use the handle of a wooden spoon for mixing.
4. Taking a lime sized ball of dough at a time, flatten it to a thick disc. Using your thumb and starting at the centre of the disc press the dough outwards and shape it into a cup shape.
5. Put a spoon full of the dhal mixture into the dough cup and double over and press the edges well together to prevent splitting.
6. Steam a few at a time on a stringhopper mat.

Jelebi

250g plain flour
few drops yellow colouring
few drops rose water
oil for frying

½ tsp baking powder
300g sugar
milk
water

Preparation

1. Sieve together the flour and baking powder. Add enough milk to the flour to make a thick batter of pouring consistency. Keep aside for 10 hours in a warm place.

Method

1. Prepare a syrup by boiling the water and sugar for 5-6 minutes or until it becomes slightly thick. Remove from the heat and add the colouring and the rose water. Stir well and keep aside.
2. Heat the oil in a deep frying pan over a medium heat.
3. Put the batter in a piping bag with a 6 mm plain nozzle and squeeze onto the hot oil, making spiral shapes of about 7 cm diameter.
4. Fry until the batter turns to a golden colour. Remove from the oil and soak in the syrup for one minute.

Laddu

500g semolina
300g sugar
2 pinches cardamom powder
20g plums

100g butter or margarine
5 tbsp condensed milk
20g cadju
1 tbsp ghee

Method

1. Fry the cadju and plums in hot ghee separately and keep aside.
2. Using a large skillet roast the semolina for 10 minutes on a slow fire. Add the butter and continue roasting until the butter melts.
3. Mix in the sugar and roast for 2 minutes. Add the milk, spice, cadju and plums. Mix well and remove from heat.
4. As soon as possible and before the mixture cools shape it into lime size balls. Wet your palm with milk, to cool it down.

Mysore Paku

1 cup gram flour
1 cup water

3 cups sugar
1 cup ghee

Method

1. Dry roast the gram flour to a golden colour.
2. Make a syrup with sugar and water to a stringy consistency. While stirring continuously add small quantities of gram flour and melted ghee (alternating between the two) until all the flour and ghee have been added.

3. Cook until the mixture begins to leave the sides of the pan.
4. Spread the mixture into a greased tray and level it. Cut into squares before it cools.

Milk Rotti

3 cups raw white rice
¼ tsp baking powder
salt to taste

1 cup thick coconut milk

Preparation

1. Soak the rice in water for two hours. Drain and pound into a coarse flour. Sieve the pounded rice and retain 1½ cups of the particles retained on the sieve. Pound the rest into a fine flour.

Method

1. Mix the flour and the 1½ cups of rice particles in a bowl with baking powder and salt.
2. Add the milk and make a soft non sticky dough and knead well.
3. Form the dough into marble sized balls and flatten them into thin discs on a greased leaf or a piece of oil paper.
4. Deep fry in hot oil one at a time. While frying, spoon the hot oil over the rotti to help it puff up.
5. Fry for a minute and turn over and fry until both sides are crisp and golden brown in colour.
6. The rotti must puff up. If it does not, knead the dough well.

Mixture

2 cups gram flour
100g flaked rice
100g cadju nuts
10 green chillies (chopped)
oil for frying

200g gram dhal
200g peanuts
2 tsp chilli powder
few curry leaves
salt to taste

Preparation

1. Soak the dhal in water for 4 hours.

Method

1. Drain excess water off the dhal, pat dry and deep fry until it becomes crisp. Drain off excess oil and set aside on absorbent paper.
2. Sift the gram flour, mix well with salt and a little water to make a soft dough. Using an omappodi mould, squeeze into the hot oil. Deep fry in batches. Drain off excess oil and set aside on absorbent paper.
3. Deep fry the flaked rice until they puff up and become crisp. Drain off excess oil and set aside on absorbent paper.
4. Fry the peanuts and cadju nuts separately until they are golden in colour. Drain off excess oil and set aside on absorbent paper.
5. Fry the green chillies until crisp. Drain and place on absorbent paper.
6. Mix all the prepared ingredients and salt in a bowl. Fry the curry leaves and chilli powder in a little oil, pour over the mixture and toss well. Check and add salt if necessary.
5. Store in an airtight container.

Mothakam

1. Prepare as kolukattai but shape the filled dough into round balls.
2. If liked the stuffed dough balls could be fried in hot ghee.

Murukku

2 cups white raw rice   or
4 cups rice flour
1 tbsp sesame seeds
¼ tsp turmeric powder
salt to taste

½ cup roasted black gram flour
½ tbsp white cumin
2 cups thick coconut milk
oil for frying

Preparation

1. Wash, destone and soak the rice in water for 2 hours. Drain and pound into a fine flour.

Method

1. Mix both flours together. Mix in the sesame seeds, cumin, turmeric powder and salt. Add the coconut milk and knead into a soft dough.
2. Fill the murukku mould with the dough and squeeze into the hot oil in spiral shapes. Deep fry until both sides are crisp. Drain and when cool, store in an airtight container.

Omappodi

2 cups gram flour
1 tbsp omam seeds
pinch of asafoetida
salt to taste

1 cup steamed plain flour
(optional)
¼ tsp turmeric powder
oil for frying

Method

1. Sieve and mix the gram and plain flour (if used).
2. Powder the omam and asafoetida. Add this to the flour along with the turmeric powder and salt. Knead it into a soft dough using just enough water.
3. Fill the omappodi mould with the dough, squeeze into the hot oil in spiral shapes and deep fry until crisp on both sides.
4. Drain and when cool store in an airtight container.

Palmyrah Yam Laddu

10 palmyrah yams
½ tsp pepper
salt to taste

5 cloves garlic
1 cup scraped coconut

Method

1. Boil the palmayrah yams.
2. Break the yam into small pieces removing as many of the fibres as possible.
3. Place the yam and all other ingredients in a blender or mortar and grind them into a coarse paste.
4. Make into small balls and serve.

Palmyrah Sweet Meat

4 cups steamed plain flour or
raw white rice flour
½ tsp baking powder
oil for frying

1 bott palmyrah pulp
100g sugar
salt to taste

Method

1. Sift the flour and salt. Add the pulp and sugar to make a thick paste of dropping consistency. Mix in the baking powder.
2. Heat the oil in a deep frying pan and when the oil is hot, spoon the mixture into the hot oil using a teaspoon and deep fry to a golden brown colour turning over frequently.
3. Drain off excess oil and place on absorbent paper. Serve cold.

Palmayrah Odiyal Laddu

250g boiled odiyal flour
100g sugar or palmyrah jaggery

2 cups scraped coconut

Method

1. Mix the flour with coconut and sugar. Pound in a mortar or blend in a blender.
2. Make the mixture into lime sized balls and serve. If the mixture is too dry to form the balls add a little water.

Pagoda

See ulundu vadai (black gram) variation.

Method

1. Make the gram vadai mixture.
2. Squeeze the mixture through your fingers onto the hot oil in a deep frying pan. Fry until brown and crisp.
3. Drain off excess oil and place on absorbent paper.

Porima

2 cups parboiled rice
1 cup sugar

2 cups scraped coconut

Method

1. Dry roast the rice to a golden colour and pound it into a fine flour.
2. Blend together (or pound) the flour, coconut and sugar. Shape into small balls and serve. If the mixture is too dry to form the balls add a little hot water.

Variation

Mix together 2 cups of parboiled rice flour, 1 cup roasted black gram flour, 1 cup sugar and 1 cup roasted sesame seeds. Blend this mixture well in a blender or pound in a mortar.

Point Pedro Vadai

1 cup black gram dhal
2 cups finely scraped coconut
2 tbsp chopped onions
few curry leaves (chopped)
½ tsp turmeric powder
oil for frying

1½ cup roasted white rice flour
1 tbsp chilli powder
1 tsp sweet cumin
salt to taste

Preparation

1. Soak the dhal in water for 5-6 hours. Wash and drain.

Method

1. Put the drained dhal along with all other ingredients into a bowl and using boiling water mix into a stiff coarse paste.
2. Take a tea spoon full of paste and shape it into a ball, partially dip in oil and flatten into a disc on wax paper or a polythene.
3. Deep fry the discs in hot oil until crisp, turning over frequently.
4. When cool store in an airtight container.

Seeni Ariyatharam

4 cups white raw rice
½ tsp baking powder

salt to taste

2 cups sugar
little thick coconut milk
or condensed milk
oil for frying

Preparation

1. Soak the rice in water for 2 hours. Pound it into a very coarse flour. Sieve it and set aside 2 cups of small particles retained on the sieve.
2. Continue pounding the rest of the rice particles into a fine flour.
3. Mix the flour, rice particles (2 cups), sugar, salt and the baking powder in a bowl. Moisten the mixture with the milk, mix well and set aside for 4 hours.

Method

1. Knead the dough well.
2. Heat the oil in a deep frying pan over a low fire. When the oil is hot take marble sized balls of dough, flatten them between your greased palms and deep fry them to a golden colour on both sides

Sesame Balls

500g sesame seeds
125g roasted parboiled rice flour

250g palmyrah jaggery
125g roasted black gram flour

Preparation

1. Wash and destone the sesame if required.
2. Drain the excess water and lightly pound or mash the seeds and sun dry. After two hours of drying crush the seeds by hand, winnow out the husk and dry again. Repeat until the sesame seeds are quite dry and crisp.

Method

1. Pound the dry sesame seeds into a powder.
2. Mix the gram flour and rice flour. Gradually add it to the sesame powder and continue pounding.
3. Once all the flour has been added pound in the jaggery until the mixture becomes a thick sticky and oily paste.
4. Make the paste into lime size balls and serve.

Hint: Store the balls in a container. They will keep for a month

Sippi

2 cups plain flour
¼ tsp baking powder
1 cup sugar
oil for frying

4 tbsp ghee
½ cup water
salt to taste

Preparation

1. Sift the flour with baking powder in a bowl. Add the ghee and salt to the flour and mix well. Make it into a firm dough by mixing with a little water. Knead well and leave it for an hour.

Method

1. Split the dough into marble sized balls. Taking one ball at a time, place it on the prongs of a fork. Press the dough ball downwards and away from the fork. The dough will become lightly groved and curl up like a sea shell.
2. Deep fry the rolled dough in hot oil stirring occasionally until crisp and golden brown in colour.
3. Make sugar syrup of stirring consistency by boiling sugar and water. Test the thickness of the syrup by dropping a little syrup into cold water. The syrup should solidify.
4. Remove the syrup from the fire and pour over the cold sippis and toss well to coat the sippis with the sugar syrup.

Sundal

250g kadalai
4 red onions (sliced)
½ tsp sweet cumin
½ cup small coconut pieces
salt to taste

3 dry chillies
sprig of curry leaves
½ tsp mustard seeds
1 tbsp oil

Preparation

1. Soak the kadalai in water for 10 hours.

Method

1. Wash and boil the kadalai in water until soft. Add the salt and cook for a further 3 minutes. Drain and set aside.
2. Fry the onions, broken chillies and curry leaves in hot oil. Once the onions are browned add the cumin and mustard and fry for a minute.
3. Mix in the boiled kadalai and coconut pieces. Sauté for a minute, remove from heat and serve hot.

Ulundu Vadai (Black Gram)

2 cups black gram dhal
5 green chillies (chopped)
3 cm piece ginger (finely chopped)
salt to taste

1 big onion (chopped)
1 tsp sweet cumin
sprig curry leaves
oil for frying

Preparation

1. Soak the dhal in water for 6 hours.

Method

1. Wash and grind the dhal to a smooth thick paste. Mix in the onions, chillies, ginger, crushed cumin, chopped curry leaves and salt.
2. Make the paste into lime sized balls, flatten to 1 1\2 cm thick discs and make a hole in the centre of each.
3. Deep fry in hot oil until they are golden brown in colour. Drain off excess oil and serve with coconut chutney.

Variation

Gram Vadai: Instead of black gram dhal use gram dhal and grind into a coarse paste. Mix with other ingredients and make into the balls, flatten slightly and fry without making a hole.

Curd Vadai

Method

1. Make vadais with 1 cup black gram dhal and soak in hot water for 5 minutes. Squeeze out excess water from the vadais.//
2. Beat 4 cups of curd and soak the vadais for 30 minutes. Then sprinkle 1 tea spoon of chilli powder and salt over the curd vadais.
3. Fry ¼ tsp of asafoetida, ½ tsp of mustard seeds and a few curry leaves in 1 table spoon of oil and pour over the vadais before serving.

REFRESHMENTS

Jaggery Water

2 bottles water
or chilled water

100g jaggery
2 limes

Method

1. Dissolve the jaggery in the water. Squeeze and mix the juice from the two limes. Strain and serve.

Morr

2 cups curd
3 red onions (finely chopped)
2 green chillies (finely chopped)

5 cups water
½ lime
2 pinches salt

Method

1. Beat the curd.
2. Mix the onions, chillies and salt and mash lightly. Add the curd and lime juice, mash again.
3. Pour the water and mix well before serving.

Variation

Instead of the lime juice a pickled lime could be mashed in with the onions and chillies. Omit the salt.

Uurukai Water (Pickled Lime)

1 pickled lime
2 red onions (chopped)
1 green chilli (chopped)
1 bottle water

Method

1. Thoroughly mash the lime, chilli and onions. Mix with water or blend all the ingredients together in a blender.

Sweet Palmyrah Toddy

3 bottles sweet palmyrah toddy
1 raw mango

Method

1. Peel and finely chop the mango and mix with the strained sweet toddy. Chill and serve.

Variations

1. Boil the sweet toddy for an hour or until it becomes light brown in colour. Keep aside for 2 hoursfor the sediment to settle. Strain and serve.
2. Cook 2 cups raw rice with water till soft. Add one cup thick coconut milk and boiled, strained palmyrah sweet toddy. Bring to boil and simmer for 10 minutes.
3. This porridge is very sweet and has a pleasant fragrance. Serve hot or cold.

Young Coconut Water

1 young coconut lime juice
sugar to taste

Method

1. Cut the young coconut and pour the water in a glass. Scoop out the kernel and add to the coconut water and serve. Alternatively chill the young coconut. Then cut and serve as above. Add a little lime juice and sugar before serving.

Young Palmyrah Fruit

2 young palmyrah fruits

Method

1. Choose young tender fruits and cut off the top. Scoop out the pulp and juice from the fruit and eat. This is very delicious.

CAKES AND PUDDINGS

USEFUL BAKING TIPS

* Cooking times may vary depending on the efficiency of the oven.
* Always preheat the oven to the specified temperature before placing the food in.
* Dishes should always be placed in the centre of the oven unless otherwise stated.
* Cake mixtures should be baked as soon as they have been prepared. They should not be left to stand.
* If the top of the cake browns before the cake is baked, cover with a double fold of ordinary paper and continue cooking.
* To ascertain if the cake is done, thrust a skewer into the centre of the cake and withdraw it. The skewer should come out clean.
* The oven door should not be opened for at least 5 minutes after placing the cake inside. Avoid opening the door frequently.
* Cakes should be cooled on a wire rack.
* Always sieve the flour, icing sugar and cocoa powder.
* Rub dried fruits, candied peel and glacé cherries in flour before adding them to the cake mixture. This will prevent them from sinking to the bottom of the cake and ensure that they are evenly distributed within the cake.
* All spoon measurements used in these recipes are level unless specified otherwise.
* Oven temperatures

Very cool	Mark 1	275°F	140°C
Cool	2	300°F	150°C
Moderately cool	3	325°F	170°C
Moderate hot	4	350°F	180°C
Moderately hot	5	375°F	190°C
Hot	6/7	400-425°F	200-220°C
Very hot	8/9	450-475°F	230-240°C

* If self raising flour is not available, for every 100g plain flour add a level tea spoon of baking powder and sieve together.

Lining and Greasing Cake Tins

All tins except non stick types must be greased. The need to line cake tins is very much dependent on the recipe. For fruit cakes the sides as well as the base of the tin needs to be lined using a double thickness of grease proof paper.

Greasing the Tin

Brush the inside of the tin with melted butter, margarine or oil. If the tin is not being lined dust it with flour. To dust the tin with flour place some flour in the tin and move it around the tin to make the flour stick to the fat. Discard the excess flour.

Lining a Round Tin

Place the tin on two layers of grease proof paper. Using a pencil draw around the circumference of the tin and cut out the two pieces of circular paper.

Next cut out a strip of paper 2½ cm wider than the depth of the tin. The length should be slightly longer than the circumference of the tin.

Take this strip of paper draw a line 2½ cm away from one of the long edges and fold along that line. Snip this 2½ cm wide strip at 3 cm intervals. The cut should extend up to the line and be at an angle to the line.

Grease the tin. Place one of the circles of paper in the bottom of the tin, followed by the paper strip with the slit side down. Push the paper right down and fold the slit strip over the base. Place the second piece of circular paper on the bottom of the tin to cover all the slits. The tin is now lined.

Lining Rectangular and Square Tins

Draw the base of the tin on grease proof paper and cut out the shape.
Cut another rectangular/square grease proof paper. The length of this paper should be equal to the length of the tin plus twice the depth of the tin. The width should be the width of the tin plus twice the depth of the tin.
Centre the tin on this larger piece of paper. Starting at each corner of the paper cut the paper up to the nearest corner of the tin. Repeat this for all four corners of the paper.
Grease the tin and both pieces of grease proof paper. Place the larger paper such that the uncut part of the paper lies on the base of the tin. Now fit the paper around the sides.
Once done place the smaller piece of rectangular/square paper on the base.
The tin is now lined.

Lining Swiss Roll Tins

Grease and line a shallow tin. Line the sides of the tin with paper at least 4 cm longer than the tin, cutting into each corner.

Lining Loaf Tins

The method is same but the paper should be 15 cm higher than the top of the tin.

Butter Cake

450g butter or margarine
450g flour
4 tsp baking powder

450g sugar
8 eggs
2 tsp vanilla

Method

1. Oven setting 180°C/350°F/Gas mark 4
2. Grease and line a 36 cm x 25 cm cake tray with grease proof paper.
3. Sift the baking powder and flour together.
4. Using a mixer cream the butter and sugar into a smooth cream. Continue beating and add the eggs one at a time.
5. Turn the mixer over at slow speed and incorporate the flour into the cake mix one table spoon at a time. Do not beat the mixture. Once all the flour has been added pour in the vanilla and mix.
6. Place the mixture in the prepared tray and bake on the middle shelf of a preheated oven for 45 minutes. Do not open the oven door for the 45 minutes. After 45 minutes and when the cake is firm to the touch, remove from the oven and turn it on to a wire rack. Remove the lining paper and allow it to cool.
7. Decorate with butter icing if preferred.

Variations
Lemon/Orange Cake: When mixing the flour add very finely grated rind of two lemons or one orange and the juice.
Chocolate Cake: Take out 4 table spoons of flour and add 4 table spoons of cocoa powder. Sift together and mix in the butter cream.
Fruit Cake: Add chopped fruits with the flour. Rub a little flour around the fruits before adding them to the mixture.

Butter Icing

125g butter
2 tbsp milk

225g sifted icing sugar
2 tsp vanilla (see flavours)

Method

1. Beat the butter with a little icing sugar until it becomes smooth. Add the remaining icing sugar, milk and vanilla, beat to a creamy texture.
2. This icing is sufficient for a 20 cm sandwich cake.

Flavours:

Lemon/Orange: Add the grated rind of a lemon/orange and replace the 2 tbsp of milk with 2 tbsp of lemon/orange juice. A few drops of lemon/orange colouring will add colour to the icing.

Chocolate : Blend 1 table spoon of cocoa powder with 2 table spoons of boiling water. Allow to cool and add this to the mixture together with 1 table spoon of milk.

Coffee: Replace 1 table spoon of milk with 1 table spoon of coffee essence.

Peppermint : Add 1 tea spoon oil of peppermint to the milk before blending with creamed butter and sugar. Colour it pale green.

Rum : Add a few drops of rum essence or 1 table spoon of rum to the milk before blending and colour it with a few drops of gravy browning.

Sponge Cake

3 eggs
75g plain flour
140g castor sugar
icing sugar

Filling

150 ml double cream (whipped) 2 tbsp strawberry jam

Method

1. Oven setting 190°C / 375°F / Gas Mark 5
2. Cut the oil paper to fit a 23 cm round cake tray, smear the paper with butter or margarine and line the tray. Sprinkle a little flour around the tray and toss the flour around. Remove all excess flour.
3. Whisk the eggs and sugar using an electric beater until all sugar has dissolved and the mixture is thick enough to leave a trail. Alternatively beat by hand but place the bowl over a pan of boiling water while beating.
4. Fold in the flour, then pour into the prepared tray and bake in a preheated oven for 35-45 minutes until the cake springs back after being lightly pressed.
5. Turn on to a wire rack to cool.
6. Split the cake into two halves (2x 23 cm discs) and sandwich together using jam and cream. Sprinkle icing sugar over the top of the cake.

Fruit Cake II

225g self raising flour
100g margarine
1 tsp finely grated orange rind
1 egg beaten

pinch of salt
90g castor sugar
150g mixed dried fruits
6-7 tbsp milk

Method

1. Oven setting 180°C/ 350°F/ Gas Mark 4
2. Grease and line a 450g loaf tin or 15 cm round tin.
3. Sift the flour and salt into a bowl. (If it is plain flour, add 2 tsp of baking powder and sieve) Rub in the margarine.
4. Add the sugar, fruits, orange rinds and toss all the ingredients together. Add in the egg and milk, stir briskly to make a semi stiff batter.
5. Transfer to the prepared tin and bake just above the centre of a preheated oven for 1 to 1¼ hours. By this time the cake should have risen well and a skewer inserted into the middle of the cake should come out clean. If not continue baking for a few more minutes.
6. Remove from the oven and allow to cool in the tin for 20 minutes. Turn out onto a wire rack to cool completely and remove the lining paper before serving.

Dundee Cake

150g margarine
225g self raising flour or plain flour with 2 tsp baking powder

150g sugar
3 eggs
25g-50g blanched almonds

350g mixed dried fruits 50g glacé cherries
50g chopped candied peel little milk

Method

1. Oven setting 160°C /325°F / Gas Mark 3
2. Line and grease an 18x20 cm cake tin. Sift the flour.
3. Cream the margarine and sugar into a fluffy mixture. Beat in the eggs one at a time. Fold in the flour, fruits, cherries, peel and enough milk to give the batter a soft dropping consistency.
4. Pour into the prepared tin and cover with almonds. Brush the almonds with egg white and bake in the centre of a preheated oven for about 1¾ hours. If the cake browns too quickly (check through viewing panel) turn the heat down slightly after about an hour of baking.

Lemon Pudding

1 tbsp sago 1 egg
3 cups milk 2 tbsp jaggery
3 tbsp sugar 3 drops lemon essence

Method

1. Boil the sago with the milk. Remove from the fire.
2. Add the jaggery, sugar, beaten egg and lemon essence. Mix well, pour into a bowl and steam or bake in a moderate oven for 45-50 minutes.
3. Leave to cool and chill for several hours before serving.

Rich Cake

225g butter
225g semolina
1 tbsp black treacle

1½ tsp mixed spice
2 grated orange rind
125g chopped cadju or almonds
175g raisins
125g candied peel
125g ginger preserve
2 tsp almond essence
1 tbsp bees honey

6 eggs
250g dark brown sugar
100g ground cadju or almonds
2 grated lemon rind
¾ tsp grated nutmeg
450g currants
300g sultanas
125g cherries
2 tbsp orange juice
2 tsp rose essence
3 tbsp brandy

Preparation

1. Wash and dry the currants. Stone and cut the raisins into small pieces. Wash and stem the sultanas.
2. Finely chop the candied peel. Cut the cherries and the ginger into small pieces.
3. **Dry all the washed fruits thoroughly. Wet fruits will sink to the bottom of the cake.**
4. Mix the fruits, nuts, spice, rinds, bees honey, half of all the essences and half the brandy. Cover and keep for two days.

Method

1. The flavour of this cake improves with time. The cake is best made at least one week before it is required.
2. Oven setting 150°C/ 300°F/ Gas Mark 2
3. Grease and line a 23 cm square tin with two layers of greased grease proof paper.
4. Roast the semolina slightly in 1 table spoon of butter.
5. Cream the butter and sugar into a fluffy cream. Add one egg and beat well Follow this with a spoonful of semolina and beat. Repeat five more times until all the eggs and semolina are added.
6. Mix in the treacle, orange juice, remaining essences, remaining brandy and the fruit mixture, mix thoroughly. It may be easier to mix these in one at a time.
7. Stir in the remaining semolina and spread the mixture into the lined cake tray. Make a slight hollow in the centre of the cake so it will be flat when baked.
8. Wrap the outside of the cake tin with 2 layers of brown paper and bake in the centre of a preheated oven for 3 hours. Check if the cake is cooked by pushing a skewer into the centre of the cake and seeing if it comes out clean.
9. As soon as the cake is baked remove from the oven and allow to cool in the tin. Once cooled turn onto a wire rack and remove the lining paper.
10. Wrap the cake in wax paper and foil before storing. The cake can be stored for up to 2 months.

Chocolate Fudge Cake

200g plain flour
1 tsp baking powder
150g soft brown sugar
2 eggs
300 ml milk
For Chocolate Icing
175g plain chocolate
To Decorate
75g chocolate sugar strands

1 tsp bicarbonate of soda
1 tbsp cocoa powder
2 tbsp golden syrup
150 ml vegetable oil

2 tbsp single cream

Method

1. Oven setting 160°C/ 325°F/ Gas Mark 3
2. Grease and line a 23 cm cake tin.
3. Sift the flour soda, baking powder and cocoa powder into a bowl. Make a well in the centre of the flour mixture and pour in the sugar, syrup, eggs, oil and milk. Beat into a smooth mixture.
4. Pour into the prepared tin and bake in the centre of a preheated oven for 45-50 minutes. Remove and leave in the tin for a few minutes before turning out onto a wire rack.
5. Heat the chocolate and the cream very gently in a small pan. As soon as the chocolate has melted remove from the heat, cool slightly and pour over the cake
6. Decorate with the chocolate sugar strands.

Swiss Roll

3 eggs
75g self raising flour
4 level tbsp warmed jam

125g castor sugar
1 tbsp hot water
castor sugar for dredging

Method

1. Oven setting 200°C /400°F /Gas Mark 6

2. Line and grease a 18 x 28 cm Swiss roll tray.

3. Whisk the eggs and sugar using a electric beater until the mixture is thick enough to leave a trail. Alternatively beat by hand but place the bowl over a pan of boiling water while beating.

4. Fold in flour and water, then turn into the prepared tray and bake in a preheated oven for 8-10 minutes.

5. Turn the baked cake onto a sugared oil paper. Peel off the lining paper used for baking and trim the edges of the cake to make a rectangle.

6. Cut out a wedge of cake (paralell to the short edge and 2/3 of the depth of the cake) about ½ cm away from one of the short edge nearest you. Spread with the jam and roll up quickly and tightly starting from the edge where the wedge of cake was cut out.

7. Hold in position for a few minutes then cool on a wire rack. Dredge with castor sugar before serving.

Hints on baking : If plain flour is used add ½ tsp of baking powder to it.

Variation

Chocolate Swiss Roll: Replace 1 level table spoon of flour with 1 level table spoon of cocoa powder and bake as above. Use whipped cream as a filling or chocolate icing.

Mocha Hazelnut Gateau

175g butter or margarine
150g self raising flour or
1½ tsp of baking powder with plain flour
1 tbsp cocoa powder
40g finely chopped hazelnuts

175g castor sugar
3 large eggs

1 tbsp coffee essence

Filling

350g butter
1½ tbsp coffee essence
few whole hazelnuts (to decorate)

600g sieved icing sugar
4 tbsp chopped hazelnuts

Method

1. Oven setting 190ºC/ 375ºF/ Gas Mark 5
2. Grease and flour two 20 cm sandwich tins.
3. Cream the butter and sugar into a smooth mixture. Beat in the eggs one at a time. Fold in the flour and cocoa powder. Add the nuts and coffee essence.
4. Turn into the prepared tins and bake in the centre of a preheated oven for 20-25 minutes until the cake is firm to the touch.
5. Remove from the oven and turn onto a wire rack before allowing it to cool.
6. Make the filling by creaming the butter with sugar and coffee essence.
7. Use a quarter of the filling to sandwich the two cakes. Use a quarter to cover the sides. Roll the side of the cake in the chopped nuts to coat the icing with nuts.
8. Spread some of the remaining icing on the top of the cake and use the remainder of the icing to pipe rosettes on to the cake. Decorate the top with whole nuts.

Cheese Cake

175g digestive biscuits
700g cream cheese
1 tsp vanilla
3 eggs (separated)
finely grated rind and juice of a lemon

50g melted butter
175 castor sugar
2 tbsp corn flour
150 ml double cream

Method

1. Oven setting 160°C/ 325°F/ Gas Mark 3

2. Grease a 20 cm round tin with a detachable base (spring form).

3. Crush the biscuits, mix it with melted butter and press it in to cover the base of the prepared tin. Chill for 30 minutes.

4. Beat the cheese, lemon rind, juice, sugar, vanilla, corn flour and egg yolk together to form a smooth mixture.

5. Separately beat the egg white until stiff and the cream until it is thick.

6. Fold into the cheese mixture the egg white and cream. Add a spoonful of egg white followed by a spoonful of cream and so on. Use a large metal spoon to fold.

7. Put the mixture into the prepared tin and bake in the centre of a preheated oven for 45 minutes. Turn off the heat, open the oven door and allow the cake to cool in the oven for 30 minutes.

8. Take out the cake from the tin and chill before serving.

Variation:

Flavour with ½ tsp of mixed spice instead of the vanilla and lemon.

Place firm fresh fruits such as cut strawberries, diced pineapple, halved apricots etc. on the biscuit base before filling with cream.

Orange Cheese Cake

175g digestive biscuits
4 tbsp castor sugar
100 ml water
½ lemon
150 ml single cream

50g butter(melted)
2 tbsp gelatine
2 oranges
225g cream cheese

Method

1. Grease a 20 cm round tin with a detachable base. (spring mould)
2. Crush the biscuits, mix it with melted butter and press it in such that it covers the base of the prepared tin. Chill for 30 minutes.
3. Dissolve the sugar in water and heat over a low fire. Sprinkle the gelatine and stir until it is dissolved. Leave to cool for 10 minutes.
4. Meanwhile peel the rind from a orange, dice finely and add to the syrup.
5. Squeeze the juice from the lemon and oranges. If the total volume of juice is less than 175 ml add more orange juice to make up 175 ml.
6. Put the syrup, cream, citrus juice and half the cheese in the blender and blend into a smooth mixture.
7. Add the rest of the cheese and blend for one more minute to make a very smooth mixture.
8. Pour into the prepared tin, refrigerate until set. Garnish with candied peel before serving.

Candied Peel

1. Wash the citrus fruits to remove the waxy coating.

2. Cut strips of the skin and discard the pith (white part).

3. Boil the strips in water for 5 minutes, drain and rinse.

4. Put equal amounts of granulated sugar and golden syrup by volume. Cover this mixture with a layer of water. Bring to the boil over a slow fire making sure that it does not caramalise (burn). Turn off the heat.

5. Soak the boiled peel in the syrup for 30 minutes. Cool the strips on a wire rack, roll in sugar and leave to dry.

Doughnuts

225g self raising flour or plain flour with 2 tsp baking powder
1 egg
6-7 tbsp milk and water
oil for frying

pinch of salt
2 tbsp melted butter or oil
50g sugar
jam
sugar

Method

1. Sieve the flour and salt. Thoroughly mix in the butter or oil, egg and sugar. Gradually mix in the milk to make a soft dough. If the dough is sticky leave it to stand for 10 minutes.

2. Roll the dough out onto a lightly floured board and cut into rings. Alternatively roll them into small balls, make a hole in them with your finger, fill the hole with the jam and roll the balls again to seal the jam.

3. Heat the oil in a deep frying pan, slide in the shaped dough and fry to a golden brown colour turning them over.

4. Remove from the oil, drain off the excess oil and roll it in sugar.

Cream Buns

60g self raising flour
25g butter or margarine
1-2 eggs
1 tsp castor sugar
icing sugar

pinch of salt
½ cup water
½ pint double cream
½ tsp vanilla

Method

1. Oven setting 220°C/ 425°F/ Gas Mark 7
2. Grease 2 round shallow biscuit tins about 25 cm in diameter with well fitting lids. If not available, use greased roasting tins closely covered with foil.
3. Bring the fat and water to the boil in a small pan. Remove from heat, add all the flour at once and mix briskly to form a ball of dough.
4. Add the egg and beat until it is absorbed. If necessary add a little more beaten egg such that the mixture can be pulled up into soft points with a spoon. Continue beating until the mixture becomes smooth.
5. Taking one teaspoon of mixture at a time, place them 5 cm apart in both tins. Each tin should hold about 7 teaspoons of mixture.
6. Close the lids of the biscuit tins. Place them one on top of another and bake in a preheated oven for 45 minutes. Reverse the position of the tins half way through baking.
7. Beat ½ pint of double cream, mix in the sugar and vanilla. Cut the buns in half, fill the base with cream and replace the top half. Dust the icing sugar over the buns and serve.

Variation:
The buns can be filled with ice cream, fresh fruits or whipped cream.

Chocolate Eclairs

50g butter or margarine
pinch of salt
2 large eggs
1 dess sp cocoa powder
150g icing sugar
½ tsp vanilla

¾ cup water
90g plain flour
whipped cream
4 tbsp water
small knob butter

Method

1. Oven setting 220°C/ 425°F/ Gas Mark 7
2. Grease a baking tray.
3. Place the water, salt and margarine in a pan and slowly bring to the boil. Once boiled add all the flour and beat until the mixture begins to leave the side of the pan. Remove from the heat.
4. When cooled beat in the eggs one at a time.
5. Using a piping bag with 1.2 cm plain nozzle, pipe 10-12 cm lengths of the mixture onto the baking tray.
6. Bake for 25-30 minutes in a preheated oven. Remove from the oven and cool after slitting the eclairs down the side.
7. Once cooled fill with whipped cream and coat the top with chocolate icing.

Chocolate Icing

8. Blend the cocoa and water. Cook this until it thickens and add the butter to it. Allow to cool.
9. When cooled mix in the icing sugar and vanilla. The mixture should be thick and be of coating consistency.

Pineapple Cream

1 tin ideal milk
4 tbsp hot water
350g canned pineapple
vanilla

4 tsp gelatine
4 eggs
6 tbsp sugar
yellow colouring

Method

1. Beat the eggs with the sugar. Add in the milk, beat and cook (stirring continuously) on a slow fire until the mixture thickens. Remove from the fire and cool.
2. Drain the syrup from the pineapple pieces. Save the syrup and chop the pineapple pieces.
3. Dissolve the gelatine in hot water and add it to the cold milk mixture with the vanilla. Follow this with the pineapple pieces and syrup mixing them well in. Add the colouring .
4. Pour into the serving bowl and chill until set.

Pineapple Pudding

100g margarine
100g flour
1 canned pineapple
1 tsp vanilla

100g sugar
2 eggs
1 tsp baking powder

Method

1. Sieve the flour with the baking powder.

2. Drain the syrup from the pineapple pieces. Save the syrup and chop the pineapple pieces.

3. Cream the margarine with the sugar. Beat in the eggs one at a time. Fold in the flour and then mix the chopped pineapple pieces.

4. Pour the mixture into a greased bowl and steam for 45 minutes or until it is firm to the touch.

5. Serve hot or cold with the pineapple syrup.

EggLess Fruit Cake

450g mixed dried fruits
225g margarine
2 cups strong tea
2 tsp bicarbonate of soda

450g flour
225g sugar
2 tsp mixed spice

Method

1. Oven setting 160°C/ 325°F/ Gas Mark 3

2. Grease and line a 20 cm square cake tin.

3. Clean, stone and cut the fruits into small pieces.

4. Place the chopped fruits, margarine and tea in a heavy bottom pan, bring to boil and boil for 2 minutes. Remove from the heat and allow to cool.

5. Sift the flour with bicarbonate of soda and add it to the cold fruit mixture together with the spice. Mix well.

6. Turn the mixture into the prepared tin and bake in a preheated oven for 45-60 minutes until the cake is firm to the touch.

Biscuit Pudding

200g milk biscuits
225g margarine or butter
4 tbsp cocoa powder
4 tbsp boiling water

½ cup milk
450g sifted icing sugar
1 pineapple (chopped)
1 tsp vanilla

Method

1. Blend the cocoa powder with boiling water and cool.
2. Beat the margarine/butter with some of the icing sugar until smooth. Add the remaining icing sugar, the cocoa mixture and vanilla, beat until creamy.
3. Dip the biscuits in the milk one by one and cover the bottom of a 20 cm serving bowl. Spread the icing thinly over the biscuits and sprinkle the pineapple pieces over the icing. Cover with biscuits and reapeat the same and finish with icing.
4. Chill well and serve.

Coffee Snow

2 eggs
2 tins water
1 tbsp instant coffee
2 tsp vanilla

1 tin condensed milk
6 tbsp gelatine
1 tbsp sugar

Method

1. Pour the milk into a pan along with water, sugar and egg yolks. Mix well and cook over a slow fire until it thickens. Remove from fire and allow to cool.
2. Dissolve the gelatine in half a cup of hot water and the coffee in another half a cup of hot water. Allow to cool.
3. Mix the cooled coffee and gelatine with the milk mixture. Pour into the serving dish.
4. Beat the egg whites until stiff, pour over the pudding and chill until set.